Ath

A Be

Atheism:
A Beginner's Handbook

✦

All you wanted to know about atheism and why

Philip A. Stahl,
Author of *The Atheist's Handbook to Modern Materialism*

Editor: Dr. Richard L. Stahl

iUniverse, Inc.
New York Lincoln Shanghai

Atheism: A Beginner's Handbook
All you wanted to know about atheism and why

iUniverse books may be ordered through booksellers or by contacting:

iUniverse
2021 Pine Lake Road, Suite 100
Lincoln, NE 68512
www.iuniverse.com
1-800-Authors (1-800-288-4677)

The views expressed in this work are solely those of the author and do not necessarily
reflect the views of the publisher, and the publisher hereby disclaims any responsibility
for them.

ISBN: 978-0-595-42737-6 (pbk)

ISBN: 978-0-595-87068-4 (ebk)

Printed in the United States of America

Contents

Preface vii

Introduction: When You Know You're Different 1

CHAPTER 1 The ABC's of Theism and Atheism 9

CHAPTER 2 Myths About Atheists 29

CHAPTER 3 Logical Fallacies Used on Atheists 53

CHAPTER 4 Toward An Atheist Mindset 77

CHAPTER 5 Atheists Aren't the Media's Darlings! 99

CHAPTER 6 Do You *Really* Want to be An Atheist? 105

CHAPTER 7 The Three Biggest Challenges to the Atheist 120

Resources for Atheists 129

Index 131

Preface

Since the 2000 publication of my first book on atheism[1] there has been an ongoing call for a basic text for novice unbelievers: minus most of the technical and scientific details in the original. For years, the concept percolated, awaiting the time and opportunity to bring it to fruition.

When Dr. Richard Stahl agreed to support this project, as well as convey an outline of what he'd like to see, the wheels were set into motion at full speed. The resulting book has nowhere near the heft of the original (about half the size) but I believe it more than compensates by way of understanding.

Basically, what I did is imagine the sort of information I would have liked to see if I were starting on the path to unbelief. In my case, it would have been around the age of eighteen, soon after I attended a lecture by Jean-Paul Sartre at Loyola University, New Orleans in the Fall of 1964.

In respect of my own personal experience, the exposure to Sartre's ideas got me thinking about the concepts of Being and Nothingness, as well as good faith and bad faith. Over time it became ever more apparent to me that so long as I retained religious beliefs merely for "protection" or "an afterlife insurance policy"—I was guilty of bad faith. Not being true to my own authentic self.

A book at that time would sort out the plethora of competing issues, ideas that roiled my own mind. For example, what sort of arguments for unbelief would take precedence over others? What degree of respect do unbelievers owe the religious anyway? How can the unbeliever make his own case for his non-belief devoid of emotion, hostility or aggression?

Given these parameters, what would be the approach at the most fundamental level, omitting mathematics and technical (physics) details as far as possible?

---

1. P.A. Stahl: *The Atheist's Handbook to Modern Materialism*, 2000, Professional Press.

Many ideas began to percolate, but one element of news off the wire services probably propelled the completion and book's coherence more than anything else. That was the news, in March of 2006, of a University of Minnesota study by Penny Edgell, Associate Professor of Sociology, and co-authors, Doug Hartmann and Joseph Gerteis. Their study, based on a telephone sampling of more than 2,000 households, disclosed that atheists now occupy the bottom rung of social respect for minorities in American society. They're now regarded as contemptuously as communists were in the 50s, and rated in social worth below Muslims, immigrants and homosexuals today.[2]

The study noted that a significant number of respondents associated atheism with an array of moral misbehavior, including criminality and materialist emphasis. In addition, the findings "seemed to rest on a view of atheists as self-interested individuals who are not concerned with the common good."[3] This is nothing short of astounding given that as a nation and people, Americans are notorious for giving short shrift to the "common good" as evidenced by consistently voting for no-tax or tax cutting candidates, when they know the outcome will starve government of the resources needed to advance the needs of the vulnerable, such as the 47 million currently without any health insurance.

The truer fact, that Americans may not like to confront, is that the U.S. has been committed to a rugged individualism since the country's founding. The historic confluence of free market capitalism (exalting such individualism) and evangelical Christianity probably occurred in the U.S. ca. 1885 with the publication of the Rev. Josiah Strong's book *Our Country, Its Possible Future and Its Present Crisis*,[4]

As Hofstadter notes, the acceptance of Social Darwinism in the U.S. coincided with the visit of Herbert Spencer in 1882, for a speaking tour. Spencer, for those unaware, was a British philosopher who sought to extend the principles of natural selection in Darwinian Evolution, to society as a whole. As Hofstadter points out[5], Spencer absolutely repudiated all state assistance to the poor, needy,

---

2. *University of Minnesota News*, March 31, 2006, "Atheists Identified as America's Most Distrusted Minority, According to new U of M Study."
3. Ibid.
4. See, e.g. 'The Vogue of Spencer', Chapter 2, in Richard Hofstadter: *Social Darwinism in American Thought*, American Historical Association, 1955.
5. Op. cit., pp. 41-42.

physically feeble, or infirm. In terms of the role of natural selection in "social evolution" such aid amounted to unwanted artificial interference in nature. Not to mention, meddling in the "natural development" of a superior society.

The Rightist-corporate elite (including many of the 'robber barons') latched on to this as a kind of dogma, and then performed another "miracle" of sorts, by blending this hyper-individualism with Christian virtue (proto-Calvinism and its work ethic), and a strict, constructionist view of The Constitution. That Americans forget this basis for rejecting the common good in the national zeitgeist, while blaming atheists for it, is nothing short of amazing in terms of hypocritical acrobatics. Or it perhaps discloses a tragic absence of historical knowledge or perspective.

In general, the respondents believed they "shared a basic sense of moral right and wrong" with everyone but atheist fellow citizens. Difficult to comprehend when the bulk of those in prison for major felonies are members of one religion or the other! And this study emerged after more than 30 years, during which Americans have been led to believe by their media that the seeds of social tolerance had finally sprouted.

The sheer scope of the revealed ignorance cried out for disclaimer and, most of all, a basic and fundamental brief for the defense of all atheists everywhere. That Americans, who prided themselves as being inheritors of the principles of liberty from John Stuart Mill, Franklin, Jefferson and others, could descend to such an abominable level of prejudice was appalling in itself. That it could manifest in the 21st century was even more outrageous.

The resulting response to this demeaning collective attitude of fellow citizens is this basic handbook, which I believe will hold great value to younger and older atheists alike, especially those who may have been put off by the original, more technical work. I'm hoping this basic finds wide circulation within the atheist community, and also serves as a touch point for further advocacy and the teaching of atheist positions.

I'm also hoping, but not too optimistic at the present time, that at least some of my compatriots that share the hostile attitudes revealed in the University of Minnesota study will take the opportunity to open their minds, if even a crack.

To at least achieve some semblance of comprehension of what they are inveighing against, before they similarly respond to a future study.

Of course, author Morris Berman has noted another, more depressing alternative: that graciousness, tolerance and humanity may no longer be possible in a nation (in the words of Nicholas von Hoffman) rife with a collection of "asses, dolts and blockheads."[6] A people that choose to live in a self-fabricated fantasyland, or a bubble cut off from all reality. The question is why any sane, rational and well-informed atheist should take a cue from such a forlorn lot or allow their prejudices to dictate future behavior.

Finally, there will be many ideas, concepts and illustrations presented in this book. It is possible that a majority of these will be unfamiliar to the general reader or beginner atheist. Since even cursory treatment, say in sidebars and insets, is beyond the scope of this text, I have provided ample footnotes for future reference. I encourage readers to "google" key words embodying unfamiliar concepts in each footnote. Beyond that, if possible, I encourage readers to try to get hold of the actual source text(s) referenced in the footnotes for each chapter.

Doing this will greatly enhance and amplify the benefit in reading this book, while also adding immensely to the storehouse of knowledge available to the beginning (or even mature) atheist. In today's world, one can never have too much knowledge, and being au fait with the spectrum of points and issues raised makes it more likely that any atheist will be a formidable debate opponent.

Those even more adventurous are invited to obtain my first book: *The Atheist's Handbook to Modern Materialism* and to examine the issues, detailed ethics, physics and biology concepts raised therein.

---

6.   Morris Berman: *Dark Ages America: The Final Phase of Empire*, W.W. Norton & Co. page 282. Berman cites a number of authors, including Hoffman, who agree most Americans live in a bubble divorced from reality and take their truth directly from an untrustworthy government or corporate media allied with them, rather than finding it out by their own research and independent thinking.

Introduction: When You Know You're Different

Imagine looking at a Moonless, starry sky one night. At some instant you spot a brilliant, spherical green light. It races across the sky from north to south and back then suddenly descends toward a spot on the northeast horizon. Numerous green sparkles erupt as it makes contact with the horizon.

How would you encapsulate what took place, and your reaction to it? Choose one response from the set below:

A. It's an unknown pure and simple. Not much more can be said. It doesn't convince me that there are flying saucers or visiting aliens. An unknown means exactly what it says: 'unknown

B. It was a UFO, and most likely a flying saucer. I believe this is evidence for visiting aliens.

C. It was most definitely an alien craft, and it briefly landed. I didn't see the aliens up close, but I believe they had to be continuing their observations of Earthlings!

D. Without knowledge of the sky or astronomical phenomena, it's impossible for me to make a determination one way or another. Maybe it's a saucer piloted by aliens, and maybe it's just a new form of ball lighting or meteor.

If you had chosen (A) you'd have an unbelief mindset. You don't accept or believe that the phenomenon was a spaceship from another planet. You're only prepared to say it's unknown. This is based on the fact that you also have enough knowledge of atmospheric phenomena to arrive at such a conclusion in the first place!

By contrast, if you selected (D), you'd be said to have an "agnostic" mindset. Based on your lack of knowledge of sky phenomena you acknowledge being in no position to hold either belief or unbelief. You therefore concede it may be a spaceship or, on the other hand, perhaps some known sky phenomena. You're simply not in a position to say one way or another. Your ignorance (of the sky, what's visible and when, distinguishing astronomical from manmade objects) doesn't permit you to go any further!

If you chose (B) you have a mild belief mindset. You're not inclined to go the whole hog and assert what you saw was a spaceship with aliens, but you're not prepared to reject it either. (Though you do confuse a UFO = "unidentified flying objects" with a flying saucer—which is already an identified flying object!) Thus, you take the sighting to be "evidence for visiting aliens" without a single bit of data or reports (e.g. reported radar bogeys, pilot sightings) that support it.

If you chose (C) you have a strong belief mindset. Rather than critically examine what's presented, you're tempted to take it at face value. It "looked" like some kind of alien craft, perhaps as seen in various movies you've attended, and so you conclude it's an intelligently controlled craft piloted by one or more aliens. This is despite the fact that you lack the slightest supporting evidence to make such judgment, or justify investment in the belief.

The preceding isn't merely an exercise in abstract logic or a sneak test. It's designed to show the differences in mindset of different people when faced with some unknown—devoid of being told anything about it from some outside authority. Interestingly, in the context presented—more than nine in ten people would tend to pick (A), the unbelief mode—though we know in real life this simply can't be so. Most religious people, for example, are believers, not unbelievers.

"But religion's different!" you say.

Not really. The exact same dynamic is at work. Let's say instead of the preceding example, we alter the context as follows:

Imagine a special, ancient book that has been passed down from generation to generation, translated and re-translated each step of the way. Imagine the book claims to present, as an ancient fact, that a brilliant star once appeared in the east, that three wise men followed it and were led to a special being ("alien") that was at once God and man. This being later matured, performed miracles (walking on water, changing water to wine, raising the dead, etc) and even rose from his grave to begin a new, ethereal life.

If this special book is "the bible", how would you encapsulate the events it describes, and your reaction to it? Choose one from the set below:

A. Given the fact that the first New Testament manuscripts were prepared more than forty years after the latest event depicted, it's unlikely any of the reporting is without error. To err on the side of caution, one must therefore withhold belief.

B. Even if the events were first passed along in an oral history, it is probable that most of them are true and merit belief.

C. Every last event merits belief once it has been written down. There is no issue on this score because every word is divinely inspired and must therefore be true.

D. Given the multiple translations, say Aramaic to Greek to Latin, and the editing surely done, it is impossible to say whether the events are true or not true.

Once again, choice (A) embodies the unbelief mindset, and would be characteristic of most atheists. Indeed, a savvy and knowledgeable atheist might be quick to point out that no less than a Church historian, The Rev. Thomas Bokenkotter, noted[1]:

> "The Gospels *were not meant to be a historical or biographical account of Jesus.* They were written to convert unbelievers to faith in Jesus as the Messiah, or God."

This is a shattering admission, and from a historian of Christendom's largest Church. It's a de facto admission that *no historical support exists* for any of the accounts in the New Testament. Indeed, if they "were not meant to be historical" (or accurate), then we cannot be sure if any are! Quite possibly none of the accounts should be taken seriously, and hence withholding of belief (the most basic form of atheism) is totally warranted.

---

1. Thomas A. Bokenkotter: (1992), *A Concise History of the Catholic Church*, p. 17

Meanwhile, the person who expresses choice (B) is most likely a moderate Christian. He accepts what he's told on authority, say by his pope or bishop, but isn't prepared to controvert them on his own. Who is he to question?

The person who selects (C) is most likely a biblical literalist, or what we call a "fundamentalist". There is no question on the validity of holy writ, and once in the book one accepts it since it's inerrant.

The person who chooses (D) is again an agnostic, unable to make a choice based on the lack of information (or his own inadequate knowledge base).

My point is that when one strips away the trappings and assorted incidentals, there are remarkable parallels to the "UFO" sighting example given earlier. Note that in each case, whether UFO (as a space craft) or special divine being, the atheist and his believer counterparts are totally consistent. Each time the atheist demurs and refuses to commit to any intellectual investment, and each time the believers do the opposite.

Is something more basic at work? It's possible, in fact very likely, that every human (assuming normal mental faculties) is a born atheist. He or she learns to ask questions from an early age: Why is the Sun hot? Why is the sky blue? Why does the Moon change shape? Why? Why? Why?

It's also interesting to note that no child naturally gravitates to religions, bibles or God on his own. He or she must be led in that direction by parents, teachers or others. In other words, it is society that defines and sets religious parameters and expectations.

In my own case, according to my parents, I was an extremely difficult child. Rather than pay attention at Mass I preferred to either fool around, or daydream about things imagined, or read. I recall at least one occasion where my dad actually had to drag me out of the church and give a walloping to try to correct my "un-churchly" behavior.

At the Catholic school I attended, I evidently aroused the ire of a nun in my second grade class after she directed attention to a full color picture in our religion books. The graphic depicted a male and female trapped under a grating full of flames. A mammoth demon plunged a pitchfork into their bare hides (they wore only loin cloths and their backs were presented in the text). The lesson had been intended to focus on Hell and how little boys and girls can avoid it, and I had raised my hand to ask a question.

"Yes, Philip?" the good Sister Vivina excitedly asked.

In a deadpan, I replied:

"Uh, Sister.… if Hell is so hot, how come these two still have some clothing on? Shouldn't it have been burned off along with their skin?"

The nun was flummoxed and sputtered several minutes before replying along the lines that a special place in Hell was reserved for little boys that asked such impudent questions.

But to me, it was common sense, not impudence at work. I didn't wish to make Sr. Vivina's work load more difficult, only to ascertain how it was that these flames didn't do what normal flames did—burn skin and clothing. But rather than give the budding young atheist a sensible answer, she totally cut off any inquiry—bringing up the eternal fear factor to help.

"God makes Hell much hotter for little boys that ask such questions!"

In reality, she made me despise the church's teachings even more. If the most common sense question couldn't be answered, how or why could any others? Thus, *The Baltimore Catechism* and its trite parroting became more a joke to me than anything else (though I played along in order to get promoted!)

Did Sr. Vivina or my dad ever succeed in molding me into a devout Catholic? Not at all. My upstart behavior was merely repressed and held in check. I mused silently while Mass was being celebrated, and continued to pay little or no attention. To me it was gobbledygook. I mean, ancient rituals that involved cannibalism of a man who'd been dead 2,000 years? Please!

Ditto for most religion classes, unless they dropped the dogma and addressed thought provoking questions or issues. (Which they sometimes did. For example, in one high school religion class, a question posed was whether the U.S. bombing of Hiroshima was a violation of moral precepts).

At the same time I was incredibly curious. I'd capture spiders, lizards and other critters around our home in Florida and study them for hours. When I was twelve I made my first astronomical telescope and began studying the stars, planets and nebulae. I read voraciously, and nothing in that reading or in those studies compelled me to accept that a giant being made them all or kept an eye on them.

I would submit that most if not all children are exactly the same. Left to themselves they'll ask repeated questions on everything from A to Z, conduct independent investigations of their world, and refuse to make hard and fast conclusions. Rather, like the children they are, they'll keep an open mind so long as Mom and Dad don't intervene and push their own biases, superstitions and beliefs on them!.

The problem is that Mom and Dad usually *do* intervene. Very few are liberal or generous enough to stand back, let the little ones develop, and not try to cram religious doggerel down their throats. The usual explanation given for this behavior is summed up in a response from a Christian friend of mine in Barbados:

"Well, you can't just let them go along like wild animals! You have to impart some kind of moral values and religion is the best way to do that."

In fact, this is totally mistaken, but that is material for a later chapter. For now, I will say that I have seen kids raised in totally secular households where not one word of God or Jesus or Hell is mentioned and the results were fabulous. No druggies, no gang members, no shop-lifters. What's the secret of these enlightened parents? It's very simple, actually.

Basically, if you wish your children to act in certain ways, or embrace certain values you must first *model that behavior* for them. You must model each specific behavior that you wish your children to display. You can't tell them '*Do what I say!*' or '*Listen to the priest!*' or '*Do what the Bible says!*'

You yourself have to show how a decent person lives and acts. Moreover, the decent values themselves need not be religious in any particular sense. Disdaining violence to another is not a specifically "Christian" value, but a human one. It's what a decent human does. It's the same with avoiding lying or stealing. One avoids these not because a "devil" will take one's soul at death, but because lies and theft undermine the basis for a just, cooperative and civil society. They make it a place less worth living in for all, since as one's neighbors' security is undermined, so must one's own be.

Any persistent observer of human social interaction will note that the vast majority of people are law-abiding and decent folk who naturally practice a common-sense and utilitarian ethics similar to what has been described. For proof, one need only look as far as the upstanding atheist or agnostic who inhabits every community and who—though he disdains a deity—nevertheless treats his fellows with compassion and respect. No threat of eternal punishment or commandment ordains this behavior. Instead it is the conscious and deliberate recognition that the promotion of the welfare of others is directly linked to one's own welfare.

Unfortunately, what religions have done is to take the natural code of ethics most people follow and embellish it with a blizzard of superstitious precepts and injunctions. These are superstitious since, inevitably, they are linked to the supposed dictates of a supernatural "being" who will not hesitate to "punish" those who disobey "him".

Christians, for their part, profess a "God of love", but never hesitate to invoke fear (of eternal torment) to have their morality adhered to. Logically, this suggests that the morality is insupportable without the additional imposition of some type of "divine" retribution. A punitive morality, then, is at the very core of the Christian religion. This is what one gets when religion is forced down the throats of young children. Why else drag into the picture an entire Zeitgeist that accepts as natural a place of eternal torment after death, in order to punish wrong doers?

When I cajoled my friend over this, and the real reasons for subjecting his children to religion at such a tender, impressionable age, he finally cracked and admitted:

"Yes, it's true already! I believe that bringing Hell into the mix intensifies their acceptance of moral values. I can't see any way to teach them otherwise."

There followed numerous discussions in which I showed him exactly how he might succeed. I insisted he simply model his decent behavior consistently for them every day: how he tends to his work, his respect for his wife, and how he helps her in the home and in general conducts himself as a model husband, father and citizen. This, I maintained, was all he needed to do!

To his credit, he soon shelved the religious piety and fear approach for a more authentic secular one that didn't require the bogies of Satan, Hell or demons. Only requiring self-love and self-respect. Once those were in place, in the modeling behavior process, then one naturally acquired a respect for society, for others.

Both his children, needless to say, turned out to be model citizens themselves. One is now about to graduate from Cambridge University with an advanced engineering degree, the other having established herself as a terrific singer. Both are themselves exemplars of the generous, decent behavior modeled by their parents.

What this shows is that no amount of bible punching or moralistic hectoring or even church attendance can compensate for decent parental behavior. Morality, it seems, fundamentally derives from the example demonstrated by caretakers. The important aspect here is that there is no religious component to it. An atheist can therefore produce compassionate, ethical and decent offspring as well as his Christian, or Jewish counterparts.

This is the basic and central truth that people of every religious persuasion need to appreciate, while eliminating the bigotry and false assumptions that drive their distrust of those with different beliefs. Or those with no beliefs at all.

Summary concepts:

1. Belief is contingent on face value acceptance as opposed to critical analysis.

2. UFOs are a simple example and religious claims bears many parallels to them

3. Children are all born rationalists, not religionists, hence born atheists.

4. Children learn best by decent parental behavior modeled for them, not by hectoring them with hellfire threats for misbehavior.

1

The ABC's of Theism and Atheism

○ ○
"God is a concept by which we measure our pain."

—John Lennon

1. From Natural Gods to Theism

The tendency to posit a superior being or power to account for physical existence is nearly universal in every human culture. For one thing, it appears the need or desire to worship something greater than ourselves is hard-wired into our brains. Perhaps the first object of worship for the majority of humans, before the advent of language and the power of abstraction, was the Sun.

Think about it! Here you have an object overhead, giving forth immense light and heat, on which your very life depends. Its light, moreover, helps sustain plants and that includes food crops. Without food, you perish. The warmth too, is important, since once temperatures recede too much (as they did during the ice ages) human survival is threatened.

So, the Sun figured prominently in many primitive cultures including the Egyptians, Mayans, and even the Romans. In the last case, and during the era of the Emperor Constantine, *Sol Invictus* religion dominated. The nativity of the conquering Sun was, not coincidentally, on December 25th. This is within roughly 2 days of what we now know is the winter solstice, the date on which the Sun is furthest south of the equator for a person in the northern hemisphere. The diagram below can highlight this point.

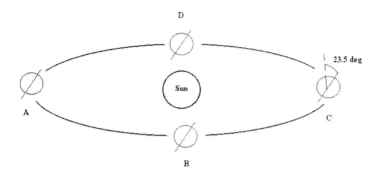

Fig. 1: The Earth's orbital path over the year. A and C represent solstices,
and C and D are equinoxes.

In Fig. 1, position C represents the winter solstice when the Sun reaches its furthest point south during the year. In the northern hemisphere the length of the day would be shortest at this point. From point C on to point D the day lengthens, so to a primitive observer, say in Palestine or ancient Rome, it would appear that the Sun has been "reborn." How could this signify rebirth?

The Romans certainly would have been adept at sky observations, and would have noted that each day past the winter solstice (C) the Sun's time in the sky grew longer. By the date of the spring equinox (point D, around March 21) that time would be nearing 12 hours. By the time of the summer solstice (point A, around June 21) it would be a maximum or over 14 hours. After the summer solstice, the time in the sky would recede again on approach to the autumnal equinox (point B). In other words, it appeared to them as if the Sun was "born" on the winter solstice, then added "life span" with each passing day until the summer solstice (A) six months later.

Not surprisingly, as Pauline Christianity gained favor in Rome and merged with Constantine's Sol Invictus cult, many key dates would be adopted. One of these remains today: the date of the Sun's "nativity" or December 25th.

As the late astronomer Fred Hoyle once noted: "Humans could do a lot worse than worship the Sun." Indeed, because if any natural object logically merited worship it was the Sun, the source of the wherewithal for life.

Of course, with the advent of language the power of abstraction grew which meant unseen entities could be substituted for the Sun. Humans realized that, because of this peculiar ability, they didn't have to limit their gods to the simply visible, physical or the known. Human imagination, indeed, emerged as the new limit. Why settle for a Sun god when one might postulate something even more magnificent, say an unseen, all-powerful and infinite entity?

With language able to fabricate at will any entity within human conception, everything was in play. Alas, the problem was that the gift of language became a curse. It enabled human imaginations to run riot in creating, inventing and promoting all manner of deities, and subsidiary agents (demons, angels, souls etc.) but without the wherewithal to back them up.

Never mind. Special books bearing the god myths (and concepts) could be written. These books were deemed "sacred" and the die was cast. Theism had been born.

2. What is Theism?

I define Theism as any form of God worship that is backed up or formalized by a sacred book or "revelation". If this last condition, especially, is fulfilled—then I say that the proposed God-concept has a theology. Theism is therefore the advocacy of a belief in a particular God-concept based on a theology.

For example, Yahweh, the Jewish deity, is set out in their sacred book, the Talmud. Thus Juadaism qualifies. So also does the Christian God, set out in the Bible, though there are various interpretations depending on which Christian sect one belongs to. Islam also qualifies, since Allah is explicated in the Qu'ran and the role of Mohammed his prophet. Similarly, Hinduism, since Brahmin is articulated in The Upanishads.

All of the above are therefore forms of Theism. That, however, is where similarities end.

To fix ideas, the typical western Christian regards his or her deity as a *personal* God, while the typical Hindu regards his or her deity (Brahmin) as *impersonal*. Even if all other things are equal, how can there be such a vast gap in human perceptions? The fact of such a perceptual chasm must mean either: a) God does not exist—at least as specified by either group, or b) God exists, but no human mind is capable of grasping even the most elemental conception accurately. Philosopher Joseph Campbell observes:[1]

> "'God' is an ambiguous word in our language because it appears to refer to something that is known. But the transcendent is unknowable and unknown. God is transcendent, finally, of anything like the name of 'God'. God is beyond names and forms."

James Byrne[2] is equally adamant:

> "The idea of God as Being is the creation of the philosophical gaze, a result of the drive to objectification which is the hallmark of the history of metaphysics. It is the 'God' which is argued about in theism and atheism, and which can only be a projection of humans."

Byrne then goes on to cite the work of French philosopher Jean-Luc Marion (from his work, 'God Without Being', 1991) who challenges people to think of G-O-D or God in a non-conceptual way. That is, only with a strike through when the word is written, to indicate no one has the capacity to describe, grasp, conceptualize or manipulate the underlying entity. In effect, as Byrne observes, "to think G-O-D is unthinkable is to reject the entire basis of onto-theology."

If then the entity is de-conceptualized it can't be debated. Note, this is a *different thing* from being "beyond knowledge" as the agnostic would define it. It is rather, beyond any capacity for human thought at all! Thus, while the agnostic can insist his position is one of "impossibility of knowledge" of God (or supernatural) this new category prohibits even writing anything.

The questions raised here go to the heart of basic theories of knowledge. How does one "know" something? And more importantly, how does one know that he knows? Or, in the absence of knowledge, does faith enter as a kind of substitute?

If Theism (which I will always capitalize) means different things to different peoples and cultures, how can one examine it with any uniformity or standards?

---

1. See: Joseph Campbell (with Bill Moyers), *The Power of Myth*, Anchor Books, New York, p. 56.
2. James Byrne, *God*, Continuum Press, 2001, p. 151.

There is one way, and that is to compare its God-concepts. If one were to take a random sample of 100 people from the phone book, and ask each to define God in his or her words, what would result?

I had occasion to do this in an informal survey prior to writing a newspaper article entitled *Science and God*.[3] In Barbados, I phoned 100 people at random and asked each to articulate his or her notion of God. Amazingly, no two descriptions matched in every respect. The most startling aspect was that fully 56 were Christians (as opposed to 6 Hindus, 8 Muslims, 10 Jewish, 18 no religion identified, 2 agnostics). Some of the responses I received:

"Jesus is God"

"Jehovah is God"

"God is love"

"God is our Father and the creator of the universe"

"God is an impersonal, physical energy."

"Yahweh is God: the I-AM-THAT-WHICH-I-AM"

"God is the principle of creativity and action"

The great diversity of conceptions of God led me to conclude that what people really meant when they professed "belief in God" was a personal allegiance to a particular *concept*. Invariably, the concept was flawed and limited because it was *abstracted* from a personal background of awareness and conditioning, as opposed to a total comprehension of *actual* being. In other words, the lack of understanding of the underlying entity (assuming there is one underlying at all) renders all concepts relative!

There is simply insufficient information to distinguish one person's concept as the "one true God" to the exclusion of all others. This means that the Jewish concept of Yahweh, the Muslim concept of Allah, the Hindu concept of Brahmin

---

3.   Barbados *NATION*, September 27, 1978, p. 14.

and the Christian concept of the Trinity all stand in the same ontological relation. From an informational point of view, none can be selected as "true" to the exclusion of the others.

Think of it! The Catholic Deity didn't exist before about 7 C.E. The Triune Deity that ushered itself into the world via a virgin, and an immaculate conception was nowhere to be found before that, except perhaps in earlier pagan tracts. The Deity that looked on each sexual transgression (e.g. masturbation, artificial birth control etc.) as a major moral offense was non-existent.

The conclusion is no less astounding for being rendered obvious: all forms of Theism are relative, or subjective. As a corollary, the faith that people express is really faith in their own concept of Theism, fashioned from their own God concept(s). There is no Theism that is uniquely true or valid, in and of itself and moreover (given the subjectivity) one form of Theism can always be totally rejected by another on the basis of "sacred text" and revelation.

This is completely analogous to there being inadequate information to distinguish one religion's claims as true to the exclusion of all others. In the case of individual religions, or religious traditions, the embodiment of the respective truth claim is found in a "sacred revelation," or holy book. For example, the Holy Bible for Christianity, the Talmud for Jews, the Koran for Muslims and the Upanishads for Hindus.

The problem is that the ancient writers, for each scripture, suffered from the same limitation of comprehension that their modern counterparts do. Their neural capacity was just as finite as that of present-day humans, and just as conditioned toward a particular conceptual allegiance. Take the account in Genesis and how it describes God's behavior: one instant creating the world and calling it "good" then becoming disenchanted and wiping it out in a flood, while bemoaning that a mistake was made. Now, a genuine God (God-*GOD*) can't make mistakes (since perfection is surely a divine attribute). However, a human brain is quite likely to project its flaws onto its own concepts. Thus, the God making the mistakes in Genesis is actually an artifact: the projection of the ancient writer's own ego onto his God concept, writ large.

Is there any advantage to acknowledging that a God-concept is what people are talking about when they use the noun "God?" I believe so. For one thing, the acknowledged use of the term God-concept reinforces the attitude of cautious forbearance mentioned earlier. The implicit relativism acts as a restraint, backing the believer away from a militant absolutism. Ideally, this should dispose him or her to be more tolerant toward unbelievers, and tolerant toward those of different religions. Far from being "wishy-washy," this affords humanity a hope that religious conflicts will one day come to an end. No more Jews versus Arabs, Catholics versus Protestants, or Hindus versus Muslims.

Far from acceding to evil, this necessary acceptance of relativity offers an escape from evil. It's an admission of intellectual humility. An admission that human brains are too limited in capacity and function to access the fundamental answers to life or to have an exclusive grasp of the "one, true God," somehow denied to all those of other faiths.

The use of the term God-concept also recognizes implicitly (by acknowledgment of a finite intelligence confronting an "infinite" entity) that the nearly universal allegiance to God-concepts is separate from the issue of a factual existence of a deity. In other words, the widespread use and appeal of God-concepts does not necessarily mean that there is a genuine correspondent in reality, supernatural or otherwise.

In fact, humanity's penchant for articulating God-concepts could be dictated by brain architecture. The prevalence of God-concepts therefore reflects certain propensities or innate characteristics associated with the brain's hard wiring, rather than an "unconscious recognition of God." One of the most compelling lines of research has been that of Michael Persinger, of Laurentian University, Sudbury, Ontario, in Canada.[4]

Persinger found that when he electrically stimulated the temporal lobes of his subjects, a "religious experience" resulted. Some of the subjects claimed to be "in contact with God" while others experienced a profound sense of unity with the cosmos, and others a feeling of immortality. None of these was an external, objective experience. All originated from the brain's temporal lobes, from electric discharges or mini-seizures that Persinger labeled 'TLTs' or temporal lobe transients. His experiments reveal, if nothing else, the human brain's complicity in inducing its own transcendent experiences. As Persinger himself has noted[5]:

---

4.   Michael Persinger.: *The Neuropsychological Basis of God Beliefs*, 1983.

"The God Experience is an artifact of transient changes in the temporal lobe."

Persinger's experiments certainly do not refute the existence of a possible, real transcendent entity, but they show that a simpler explanation is available as comports with the well-known "Ockham's Razor" principle[6]. It also shows that humans must proceed with extreme caution whenever claims concerning a deity are made. As with UFOs, the genuine signal must be separated from a vast background of interfering "noise."

3. Theology and Theism:

In the previous section, I noted that Theism is the advocacy of a belief in a particular God-concept based on a theology. So, what may we say of theology, *any* theology?

First, it's limited by what its sacred books define in terms of its "information base." Thus, no theology can concoct something in contradiction to its revelation. For example, Mary (Blessed Virgin) can't be added to the Trinity to make a "Quaternity." Jesus cannot be conceived as a pure human, non-deity. God cannot be conceived of as limited, or anything less than having ultimate attributes (omniscient, omnipresent etc.). Humans cannot be conceived as "becoming Gods" or being identified with God, or becoming "Christ" in their own right, as the Gnostics propounded.

This leaves out a wide swatch of Christian sects as having any kind of valid theology. For example, Ernest Holmes' Science of Mind (or its offshoot, Religious Science) wherein humans attain "Christhood" on their own, isn't a theology. Neither is Gnosticism, The Unity School, or Christian Science.

No theology underlies these, because each in its own way contradicts the basic tenets of the sacred source books. (Though to be fair, each of the sects would insist that it is reading the sacred book in the only correct way!) To be even more

---

5.   Persinger, M.: *op. cit.*, p. 187.
6.   The principle first articulated by William of Ockham that the hypothesis *with fewest ad hoc assumptions* is always to be preferred over the one with more. In another form it may be paraphrased as: "Theoretical existences are not to be increased without necessity."

fair, however, one may say that a definite *metaphysics* underscores all the above. By "metaphysics," I mean a philosophical formulation of the principles that don't necessarily depend upon a sacred book or dogma.

Ironically, each of the sects mentioned would be able to fit within the theology of Hinduism, since what they are proposing is analogous to the Atman relationship to Brahmin. (Each human is a spark of the divine that can activate the divine).

Second, since Theism is relative and subjective based on its (subjective) God-concepts, then all its derivative theologies and doctrines must be relative and subjective *in themselves*. This means that no theology or doctrine can be said to embody *objective knowledge*. Knowledge presumes open inquiry to obtain it in the first place, while doctrines typically foreclose inquiry *ab initio*.

If I want to investigate solar effects on Earth I first must erect numerous detectors called bolometers, to pick up the radiation incident per second. I then compare this data with other data from other, similar devices placed in different locations. Ultimately, I have used open inquiry to obtain what I need to know, and to show the Sun's effects on Earth. Thus, an item of knowledge, say that the Sun radiates 1360 watts per square meter per second, can be obtained from my inquiry.

Not so with theology! By virtue of its *dogmas* and absolutist edicts emerging from its scriptures and their interpretation, open inquiry is foreclosed at the outset. This means that the dogmas set the limits on investigations, rather than instrumental detectors or research idiosyncrasies. Stephen Hawking provides a perfect example of this in his book, *A Brief History of Time*. At the end of a (Vatican) conference on the Big Bang, he recalls being told by the Pope that he and the other astronomers were permitted to investigate the evolution of the cosmos *after* the Big Bang, but not before[7]. This is because the Big Bang itself marked the "moment of creation" and so was off limits.

Another example might be any investigations to do with the Immaculate Conception of the Blessed Virgin. The dogma of the Immaculate Conception precludes any investigations! Similarly, any purported investigation to test the

---

7.   Stephen Hawking, *A Brief History of Time*, Bantam Books, 1988, p. 122.

validity of the Ascension would be forbidden. Such investigation, after all, might find that there is minimal or no evidence for the event. That is unacceptable to believers.

4. Different Theisms:

Given the preceding section, it shouldn't be surprising that one can have different forms of Theism, but not all of these will have theologies accepted by the counterparts. The diagram below (Fig. 1) summarizes the main types of Theism:

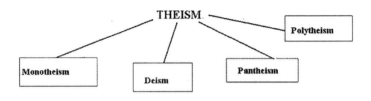

Figure. 2 The branches of Theism.

Monotheism:

Monotheism represents a belief in one deity only, though that deity may also have human attributes. Thus, Islam, Judaism, and Christianity are all examples of Monotheism. However, Christianity differs from the other two, in that it allows for a God-Man identity, and moreover a salvation role for that entity.

By contrast, Mohammed is a Prophet only, not a God-Man Savior, and Jesus is also regarded as a Prophet in Islam. In Judaism, there is neither a major Prophet (in the same central role of Jesus or Mohammed) nor a special Savior that has already arrived. Some have differentiated Christianity from Islam and Judaism by referring to it as a form of *personal Monotheism*. That is, one infinite and all-powerful God exists (or more accurately, a God-concept that articulates it!) but personal connection is afforded by an intermediary human. Thus, the infinite God is rendered a personal God.

Now, it's possible to interject additional facts here. That is, Christianity is not the *only* God-Man religion[8]. Others have existed from antiquity including forms created by the Egyptians (Horus) and the Persians (Mithras). A number of similar attributes apply to all god-man mythologies

1. A virgin mother who immaculately conceives.

2. Acclamation of the progeny as a "Son of God"

3. Reared in a foreign land.

4. He re-appears in his native land, working miracles and preaching

5. He's persecuted by his people, declared a criminal.

6. He's seized by authorities after a major betrayal, then put to death.

7. He rises from his grave, confirming he was the special divine being his disciples proclaimed

8. His followers start spreading the God-man mythology.

Take the Persian God-Man, Mithras, the Savior designated in Mithraism, who was born of the immaculate virgin Anahita, who conceived him from the seed of Zarathustra. Like Jesus, Mithras was condemned before a Tribunal but he subsequently ascended into Heaven. Mithraists recall his suffering and death with a ritual almost identical to the Communion practiced by Catholics and Anglicans[9].

This and other records from antiquity disclose that the personal God-Man foundations of Christianity are in no way unique or original but likely plagiarized by early writers from pagan sources. The degree of coincidence between so many of the actions, events (from the birth to wise men, to miracles, and suffering, Ascension) points directly to this conclusion.

---

8. For a full accounting of all "Christ" antecedents in pagan cultures and religions, see: J.M. Robertson, *Pagan Christs*, University Books, Inc., 1966.

9. Of course, all such "communions" are merely the modern revivals of the vicious, ancient rite of omophagia, e.g. devouring another human's flesh and blood to inherit his or her attributes. See, e.g. Lloyd M. Graham, *Deceptions and Myths of the Bible*, Bell Publishing Co., 1979, pp. 335-336.

This isn't what most Christians wish to hear, but one that must be considered nonetheless. Especially since it undermines the favorite refrain of so many "Believe in the Lord Jesus Christ or perish in Hell!"

Polytheism:

Polytheism represents a theology and belief in multiple deities, each of which is worshipped in turn. For the purposes of this book, I only note it here for completeness and in passing, and don't regard it as a major theistic system in today's world. So I will not elaborate on it or return to it.

Pantheism:

This holds that nature and deity are bound up as one entity—most often either as a single oneness, or in terms of the regularities of natural laws. Thus, when one worships nature one worships God, or when one appreciates natural regularities—evinced in natural laws—one is indirectly worshipping God.

In terms of crude or unrefined pantheism, the totality of the universe, its energy and all relevant fields are equated to a "divinity". This is, when one thinks about it, merely a mammoth expansion and extrapolation of Sun worship. Instead of worshipping one immediate celestial body, one is worshipping all of them as a collective.

A much more subtle form is *natural law Pantheism* which received much attention after Einstein referred to it as "Spinoza's God". When pressed to explain himself, Einstein went on to aver he didn't believe in a personal God, but rather "Spinoza's God, the order and harmony of all that exists."

In other words, the principle of regularity of natural law at work in the cosmos-elevated to a kind of impersonal deity. However, it's wise not to read too much into this, and it clearly doesn't come across as anything to be worshipped!

Much more advanced than natural law Pantheism is Emergent Holism[10]. In this case, the universe emerges as more than the sum of its parts by virtue of being "holographic". Perhaps the most important "deity" construct is David Bohm's Holomovement, a higher-dimensional "implicate order" through which consciousness is enfolded as well as matter. Bohm's "deity" at least has some scientific legs—sort of—since quantum mechanics has been used to fashion the end product. (Bohm uses a mathematical device he calls the "quantum potential".)

The Bohm Holomovement and its consequences in providing a basis for miracles and so forth, has been popularized in books such as Michael Talbot's *The Holographic Universe*. A neat thing that works out from cosmic holography, is that each and every one of us is literally a spark of the "divine". So it kind of reintroduces a form of Gnosis through the back door!

The relation of individuality to Universal Mind (Dirac Ether or Holomovement) might be depicted as I show below:

INDIVIDUAL FORMS (EXPLICATE ORDER)

___⌒___⌒___⌒___⌒___⌒___

DIRAC ENERGY SEA (IMPLICATE ORDER)

The vast energy sea or Dirac Ether is equivalent to Bohm's Implicate Order, or what he calls "Holomovement", and is a pure frequency domain[11] (timeless). The ripples on this sea are the distinct material forms perceived as separate entities in the universe because we are generally unaware of the implicate order. Nonetheless, the remarkable insight is that within this order separate forms (individualities) emerge as purely illusory. By analogy, the separate waves one sees on the ocean surface are illusions—at least in the sense they cannot be removed and placed on the beach for inspection! So also, material forms cannot be abstracted from the energy background of the Dirac Ether.

Another type of emergent deity cosmos, with pantheistic slant, was developed by Arthur M. Young.[12] Young's model treats the universe as a hypersphere torus in 4-dimensions[13]. For reference, readers can visualize this entity from the dia-

---

10. For a detailed accounting of the theories to do with this, see: *The Holographic Paradigm and Other Paradoxes*, Ed. Ken Wilber, New Science Library, 1982.

11. Frequency (F) is related to time (T) by: $F = 1/T$. Thus, $T \to 0$, for a "frequency domain".

gram below, in which I used a specific equation and computer program to generate a "Young hyper-toroid"

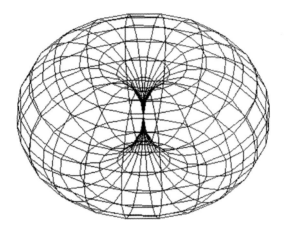

Fig. 3. A computer representation of a Young hyper-toroid

This approximates a two-dimensional analog of a Young's hyper-sphere model with the normal torus or "donut" shape with which we're all familiar. There are a number of fascinating aspects of this model. First, for the hyper-sphere with an infinitely small hole (as shown), the volume would be: $V = 2\pi^2 R^3$. Such a hyper-sphere implies an endlessly repeating universe that is the *same* in each new cycle[14]—instead of being different (i.e. with different physical constant as the reprocessed model demands). The key to this aspect is the fact that the radius R remains constant.

---

12.   Arthur M. Young: 1976: *The Geometry of Meaning*, and *The Reflexive Universe*, both published by Delacorte Press, New York.

13.   One can obtain the analogous model cosmos by taking a positive curvature, e.g. Riemann sphere, and deforming it so its opposite (north and south) poles get pulled inside until they merge at one central point.

14.   This could also be interpreted as a "timeless" universe. See, e.g. Rucker, R.: 1977, *Geometry, Relativity and the Fourth Dimension*, Dover Publications, New York, p. 105. According to Rucker: "There is no last time around or next time around because nothing is moving…we feel that we are going through time but that is an illusion."

A second intriguing aspect is that the exact same point of space-time occurs for each "beginning" (Big Bang) and "end" ("Big Crunch"). This point is easily identified in the diagram as the most constricted part of the interior "hour-glass" shape defining the inner wall of the torus-hypersphere.

Young himself attaches immense importance to the factor 2π in the hypersphere volume equation. It represents an Einsteinian curvature[15], as well as part of the uncertainty amount in quantum theory (the right side of the Heisenberg Relations, or $h/2\pi$). In the words of Young[16]:

> ... the extra 2π makes control possible. It is the entry of consciousness into the universe.

As entrancing as Young's claim is, it doesn't make any objective sense. The fact is that 2π is merely a number (2 x 22/7), nothing more or less. That it denotes "*the entry of consciousness into the universe*" amounts to a belief, not a confirmed observation, or even a hypothesis (since no tests are provided to check it). In this case, it amounts to another example of how geometry can tantalize the human brain into thinking there is an ultimate connection to transcendent reality.

Hundreds of years ago, Johannes Kepler tried to invoke the five Platonic solids, inscribed and circumscribed at definite ratios, as a geometric basis for the cosmos. Alas, he failed to find any unique arrangement of these five solids that agreed with existing astronomical observations. Ultimately, by ordering the solids in specific ways, each encased in a sphere, Kepler got a correspondence to the six known planets (Mercury, Venus, Earth, Mars, Jupiter and Saturn). However, large mathematical disparities remained apart from the fact that the discovery of Uranus and Neptune later destroyed the entire basis!

---

15. The standard Einsteinian curvature, e.g. for a gravitational background metric in the field equations, is actually $8\pi = 2\pi(4)$, so 2π represents a fraction of it.
16. Young, A.M.: 1976, *The Reflexive Universe*, Delacorte Press, New York, p. 267.

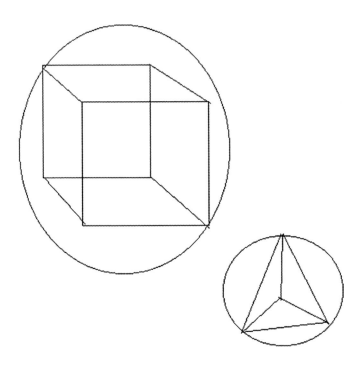

Figure. 4: Kepler attempted to use circumscribed Platonic solids to find correspondences to the 6 then known planets. When Uranus and Neptune were discovered, it became redundant.

In much the same way, there's no clear physics evidence that Young's 2π hyper-sphere has any special meaning other than that preconceived in the mind of its author. Even if we grant its validity, this doesn't mean that the cosmos emerges as a deity or deity equivalent. Nor does Bohm's Holomovement! In reality, both Young's and Bohms's efforts are purely models of the cosmos that attempt to incorporate non-physical aspects but which have been parlayed into "Gods" by over zealous followers of the New Age persuasion.

Having said that, if one were to select from the whole gamut of Gods or God-concepts, the most tolerable choice (for an atheist) would surely be pantheism in the form of Bohm's Holomovement. First, it's based on hard science (quantum mechanics and quantum field theory) and no atheist can find fault with that[17]. Second, it's pleasantly impersonal, so one's temperament isn't violated by the preposterous notion that the creative Principle of the entire cosmos became a carpenter and minor magician on one backwater planet in a primitive culture of the Roman Empire some 2,000 plus years ago. Third, there are no obligations imposed upon anyone to worship this deity under pain of "eternal torment" or even think about it. If you want to, fine, otherwise that's okay too.

Many Christians, meanwhile, find it incumbent on themselves to proselytize non-stop. They seem to need a kind of validation for their own beliefs by getting others to convert to them. Especially atheists!

What the atheist can agree on is that humanism is central to many expositions of emergent pantheism. That is, taking the best parts of these visions, such as Bohm's and Young's, and using them to enhance human potential as a cosmic agent of change. For example, making violence to oneself or others as unthinkable as violence to the planetary environment. These ideals have been cogently articulated by physicist Henry Stapp[18] as implying:

> "… a shift in the scientific conception of man from that of an isolated, accidental, mechanical epiphenomenon to that of cosmic agent with the creative power of the universe must inevitably deflate egocentric values and enhance the sense of harmonious enterprise with others, and with nature …"

Certain rationalists and non-Materialist atheists can mostly agree with the above, leaving out the part "of the universe", since that would mean the human possesses the power equivalent to a God! One may substitute for that phrase, "of one's mind", since personal mind is where creative potential begins and ends.

This is also the genesis for personal growth Christianity such as embodied in *Science of Mind* and *Religious Science*, and made popular in a number of books[19]. All these books have in common the unifying theme that evil is an illusion and each human can become a "Christ" unto himself (and indeed is an embodiment of divinity like Christ) and also that every material abundance becomes available

---

17. See: 'Quantum Theory as an Indication of a New Order in Physics: Implicate and Explicate Order in Physical Law', in David Bohm: *Wholeness and the Implicate Order*, Routledge and Kegan-Paul, UK, p. 140.

18. Henry Stapp: 1985, "Consciousness and Values in the Quantum Universe," *Foundations of Physics*, Vol.15, No. 1, p. 46.

19. See, e.g.: Ernest Holmes, *The Science of Mind*, Dodd, Mead & Co., 1938 and U.S. Andersen, *Three Magic Words*, Wilshire Book Co., 1954.

once one acknowledges that he too, is God. Their import for the atheist is that they're benign forms of Christianity that renounce the odious Heaven-Hell doctrine in favor of either cosmic unification or sequential, progressive reincarnation. In addition, they embody esoteric forms that have much in common with Eastern religions such as Buddhism.

Despite that, there is as yet no compelling evidence at all that quantum mechanics supports a holistic conception of the universe or a holistic God. The late physicist Heinz Pagels, for example, has referred to quantum measurement theory as an "information theory" and noted the entire quantum world is embedded into what we observers *can know about it*.[20] Obviously such knowledge is obtainable exclusively from observational or experiment results.

Pagels goes on to endorse the best policy in such matters as simply being a "fair witness." That means absolutely avoiding embellishment of the results or their interpretation, including projection of "fantasies." If one insists on reading more into quantum measurement results than their statistical significance allows, self-delusion ensues.

Deism:

Strictly speaking, deism treated in its orthodox and traditional manner is not Theism. Deism is, in fact, only one step removed from atheism. The only real difference is that in deism some kind of non-specific "first cause" is proposed, but after that all distinctions collapse. The atheist avers there is no one or nothing "minding the store" and so does the deist.

Deism, to give an analogy, is analogous to a child who makes a toy with a gear wheel, and the toy has the ability to move after being wound up and released. Thus, the child makes the toy (he's a clever kid) winds it up, releases it down the sidewalk, then walks away never to glance at it or its final outcome, destination. In this case, the child plays an analogous role to the ambiguous first cause of deism and the toy is analogous to the universe.

Many of the right wing, fundamentalist Christian persuasion, in order to attempt to hijack the Constitution as a "Christian document", have asserted the

---

20.   Heinz Pagels: *The Cosmic Code*, Bantam Books, pp. 162—163.

Founders were "Christians." Nothing could be further from the truth. In fact most, like Jefferson and Madison, were *deists*. The only reason this palaver gains any credibility or circulation today, is because most people (especially the lackadaisical corporate media) are ignorant of deism and so naturally are prone to conflate it with standard, monotheistic Christianity of the fundamentalist mold.

The truth is that deism is as remote from their acquaintance as wicca or some form of Eskimo aurora worship. Therein lies the tragedy, because by virtue of applying the axiom that "the squeaky wheel gets the attention," fundamentalists have managed to get millions of otherwise sober, rational people to swallow their goop.

Before fundamentalists next expatiate on the Founders, they'd do well to read the words of the letter of Thomas Jefferson to Alexander Humboldt (1813. ME 14:21):

> "History, I believe, furnishes no example of a priest-ridden people maintaining a free civil government. This marks the lowest grade of ignorance of which their civil as well as religious leaders will always avail themselves for their own purposes."

Few modern day unbelievers would dissent with this depiction. Indeed, most unbelievers would quickly agree that deists such as Jefferson are the intellectual forbears of many modern atheists, especially in terms of respecting a "wall of separation" between Church and state.

Summary points:

1. Theism has four major sub-groups, and only one of them (monotheism) is devoted to the worship of one deity. Christianity is one form of monotheism, mainly distinguished by a belief that a personal Savior, Jesus Christ, died for all humans. Christianity is not distinct in this regard, however, since numerous pagan God-Man religions predated it. A good case can be made that events from those predating pagan sources were "copped" to form at least some of what Christianity relies on for its scriptures.

2. Some forms of pantheism (e.g. Brahmin, Bohm's Holomovement) bear much resemblance to Christian holographic concepts of a "Universal Mind." Some of these forms integrate consciousness into their purview,

and try to invoke quantum mechanics to justify this. The problem is that there is no unambiguous evidence that quantum mechanics provides any such justification.

3. The atheist has no problem with such forms of "scientific" Christianity since they offer no vicious doctrines that relegate atheists to second class status in this life or any "afterlife." Indeed, these esoteric variants are more a threat to orthodox Christianity than atheism, since they posit there is no absolute evil (it's all an "illusion") and each human is himself divine[21], and hence able to become his own Christ. Hence, no exterior Christ is required for any salvation.

4. The atheist has no problem with deism since it postulates an impersonal deity that ignores its creation altogether. Deism has no special scriptures unique to itself or an ethics consistent with the type of deity it proposes.

5. All the variants of Theism reinforce the viewpoint that all God-concepts are relative and subjective. If therefore a God truly existed, it is doubtful there would be such wide divergence over Its essential nature. Theists, indeed, cannot even agree on whether their deity is personal or impersonal.

---

21. E.g. "The Key: YOU ARE GOD," in U.S. Andersen, *op. cit.*, p. 313.

2

Myths About Atheists

It isn't surprising that when you have an unpopular minority in a country, many myths will be created and propagated. For the Jews in Nazi Germany, a popular one was that they carried terrible diseases. The same is true of atheists in the U.S. today. It seems that once one admits to not believing in a God or gods, he or she becomes fair fodder on which to blame everything from the latest plague to the country's moral backslide, to just about anything else that pops into mind.

9-11? If there were no atheists knocking about, surely God wouldn't have visited this on us! AIDS? Another biblical plague sent because humans were encouraged to disbelieve, by atheists!

What makes it easier to exploit, is that there are no political stakes involved. Just about anyone can say anything he wants against an atheist, for example Michael Newdow when he went before the Supreme Court (because of the: "under God" wording in The Pledge of Allegiance), and suffer no consequences.

Political fallout? Forget it! Since the atheist mindset finds no friends or sympathizers in the Beltway, and no one really knows how many atheists vote, it isn't likely. Besides, there's little or no chance an atheist will ever achieve elected office anyway. Not in the United States of God-land! According to recent public polls, 52% of Americans would not vote for a well-qualified atheist.[1]

This is totally pathetic, and more than anything else discloses the successful incursion of anti-atheist myths into the national consciousness. What are some of these myths? Below I examine some of the most egregious one by one.

---

1.   *Mother Jones* magazine,. Sept.-October, 2004, p. 27.

1. Atheists Deny God

This is perhaps the most popular myth, because on the surface it appears to make sense. Careful thought, however, might disclose how absurd this is. For example, one generally refrains from denying anything for which belief is withheld. Let's take the example of alien colonies on the Chesapeake. Someone or group makes the claim they exist, and are planning to siphon water to take to their planet.

Fair enough. I hear the claim, but in the next breath ignore it. It is of no concern to me because it is simply too preposterous to waste investing intellectual resources. The reason is that evidence-free claims can be regarded as false or spurious until such time a modicum of evidentiary basis is provided. If this is so, it follows there is even less reason to invest precious intellectual resources to deny the claim! Why the need?

Indeed, if one *"denies"* a specious claim, he's already given it a plausible (if unconscious) underpinning. Any expenditure of mental energy in denial presumes there is at least "smoke" (if not "fire") to deny! On the other hand, if the claim is totally nonsensical, simple withholding of belief quite fits the bill and is more than adequate. As I noted in an article published in the *Mensa Bulletin, March 1994:*

> "Let's be clear about what constitutes Atheism and what doesn't. *The Atheist—to put it succinctly, absolutely withholds investing intellectual/emotional resources in any supernatural claim.* Indeed the word Atheism itself embodies this definition: *a-theos,* or without god."

What is happening here is *not active disbelief,* i.e. in making a statement *"There is no god,"* but rather simply passively withholding belief in a statement already made. Hence, the *deity believer* has made the positive claim. The ontological atheist's is the simple absence of belief in it. No more and no less. It does not and never has implied aggressive rancor or a vehement and militant opposition to the beliefs. (Though yes, some militant atheists—or what we call "strong atheists"—do have such attitudes!)

Let me quickly add here that this withholding of belief is *the more natural position*, as opposed to advocating belief, which is unnatural. Consider a different context: a neighbor runs over and informs me that aliens have landed in his yard in a spacecraft. Until I actually go over and try to verify his claim I am under no obligation to accept it as a statement of fact. Thus, the default intellectual position is always skepticism, irrespective of the claim made. This again is because the onus is always on the claimant to make good, not the skeptic to "disprove" it.

It isn't difficult to see from the above context that the more conservative (and reasonable!) position is withholding belief until a claim is validated. One does not, after all, accept a claim *then do further research*. One *ab initio* doubts the claim and then sets out to devise tests to ascertain the validity! And in the case of extraordinary claims (which certainly include "God" and visiting aliens in spaceships), "extraordinary claims demand extraordinary evidence" as the late Carl Sagan used to emphasize.

It also isn't difficult to see that this is exactly analogous to the atheist withholding belief in a deity. After all, If God genuinely exists, why is he/she/it *not uniformly perceptible*, at least in basic features, to all peoples? As we saw in the previous chapter, there are nearly as many different versions of deity as there are people. (Or at least, religions!)

This isn't surprising after all, since each person filters deity through his or her own background, knowledge, experience and perhaps even genes[2]! Thus, it is far more reasonable to make reference to "God-concepts" rather than God, just as it makes more sense to refer to an "unidentified aerial phenomenon" than a craft from another planet when one observes one or more strange lights in the sky. Caution is the byword, and withholding of belief is warranted, until proof or adequate evidence is produced.

While we're on this topic, let's consider a collateral, erroneous assumption related to this myth of denial That is, if anyone withholds belief in deity (presumed to be the Creator of the cosmos) one is obliged to come up with his or her own version of how the cosmos came to be. In fact, this is a *non-sequitur*. It doesn't follow from what's being considered.

First, it hasn't been established to the satisfaction of the skeptic that any "God" has been proven, far less that the cosmos could have been created by this

---

2.   *Psychology Today* (Aug., 1997), "Nature's Clones," by J. Neimark, p. 36.

unproven entity. Indeed, in epistemological (knowledge-basis) terms the believers haven't even gotten off first base. They have not, after all, even offered a definition of "God" in fifty words or less that can be used as a basis for practical debate. Without at least a definition, we are back to square one and Jean Luc Marion's "unthinkable G-O-D argument." In other words, the debate is ended before it's begun.

Second, and in a more general sense, the withholding of any conviction for some presumed claim (or even hypothesis) doesn't imply the skeptic must offer an entire counter-hypothesis of his own. For example, an astronomer friend may theorize that massive, invisible, dark energy particle fields are really responsible for solar flares. That doesn't mean a casual listener is obliged to take him seriously or accept his hypothesis under the proviso that if he rejects it he must arrive at his own.

Why? The mere outlandish nature of the claim is in itself enough to warrant suspicion. The listener can therefore reject it on its face, even if he knows less than nothing about dark energy or solar flares. In any case, it isn't incumbent upon him to develop a whole, entire theory of solar flares as a counter! (It is incumbent on him, perhaps, to do some follow up reading or maybe "googling" of the key issues!)

In a more prosaic case, let's say I get into an argument with a lawyer at a cocktail party. He asserts that chapter and section blah of a state contract law deems that corporations are "persons" under the 14th amendment, and hence can seize personal property if they're maligned. At most, I can give him a wink and a nod, but I'm not obliged to accept his claim even though I'm no lawyer. Moreover, I'm not obliged to arrive at my own contract case law to reject his interpretation! (I can point out that state laws of eminent domain, to my recollection, have never been invoked to the extent he claims!)

In all these cases, an unreasonable burden is placed on the skeptic merely for being skeptical. That is, that s/he is somehow not entitled to reject a claim unless a full, meticulous counterclaim can be worked up—into theory, case law or origin of the cosmos as the case may be.

2. Atheists reject morals

This is one of my favorites because it's preposterous on its face. It's also important because many otherwise sober people believe that atheists live by the rule "anything goes," since we don't acknowledge any god. On many occasions, I've been telephoned by religious types who ask: "If you don't believe in God what's stopping you from going out and raping, robbing, murdering or doing anything else? If you don't believe in God, then you don't believe in God's laws."

Invariably, I respond that decent, civilized behavior doesn't depend on god belief or adhering to 'laws' of a god. Rather, it depends on rational and objective analysis of a situation, and sound decisions maximally promoting the welfare of all concerned.

As William Provine notes, people should be encouraged to think rationally and critically concerning ethics, not out of fear of some divine force, but to protect their own long-term self-interest[3].

In line with this, any persistent observer of human social interaction will note that the vast majority of people are law-abiding and decent folk who naturally practice a common-sense, utilitarian ethics similar to what has been described. No supernatural law or commandment ordains this behavior. Instead it is the conscious and deliberate recognition that the promotion of the welfare of others is directly linked to the one's own welfare. Compromise others' security, and you in effect compromise your own. Undermine their welfare and you also undermine your own. No god is necessary.

By contrast, religious morality is predicated on some formal codification of expected human behavior in terms of absolutist propositions, not subject to debate. The typical moral code of a religionist, whether Muslim, Pentecostal, Catholic or Jewish, isn't subject to evolution or variation based on contingencies, or externalities. This blindness probably results from a "control" meme that proclaims the morality as 'god-ordained' or revealed in some scripture or other. If ordained by a god, whether Allah, Jehovah, Yahweh or whoever, it cannot be compromised or altered no matter what.

---

3. William Provine, 'Evolution and the Foundation of Ethics' (*MLB Science*, Vol. 3, No. 1, 1988, p. 25)

As an illustration of this point, despite the fact the planet is grossly overpopulated and we are approaching ecological catastrophe, the Roman Catholic Church continues it campaign against artificial birth control. Even more importantly, it prohibits its practice, under pain of grave sin, even in impoverished nations suffering in destitution from the overload.

Kai Neilsson poses it this way[4]: Is an act good because God did it, or is it good independent of such action? For a genuine ethical basis, any human action must be totally independent of whether a god did it (in scriptures) or ordains it. It must be good on its own merits. A first test, as Neilsson observes, is ethical choice predicated on a humane standard. Consider: if a human parent knows his child is trapped in a burning house, s/he will try to save it however s/he can. There is no way the human parent will simply walk out and allow "fate" or "free will" of the child to make the decision. If the human parent has an ounce of common decency s/he must intervene.

However, god-ists seem quite happy to let their deity off the hook, when and where it suits their fancy. Start then with the standard deity template, say espoused by *most* Christians. This entity is posited as both omniscient and omnipotent (all knowing and all powerful).

Let us say, as occurred back in the spring of 1994, It knew from before all time a twister was headed for its house of worship in Alabama. Being omnipotent, it also had the power to deflect said twister and let it tear up some nearby forest or woodsheds—as opposed to its church with people inside. Did it? No it did not! It permitted the tornado to demolish the church and many of those children within. All innocents. All dead.

Those who would defend such a deity but hold a human parent accountable for negligence or manslaughter by allowing their child to perish in a house fire (when the child could be saved), disclose inchoate ethics. To wit, demanding a vastly lower ethical standard of behavior for their deity than for fellow humans.

Those who beg the question with theo-babble ("*we cannot fathom the ways or mind of God*") are no better, and do no better. In many ways, they're worse,

---

4.   Kai Neilsson.: *Ethics Without God*, Prometheus Books, 1990.

because they lack even the courage to face their own logic and the consequences of their definitions! They either invoke the escape clause of "faith" or the impotence of human logic beside the alleged Divine Mind. (And surely, if humans sprung from such a mind, comprehensibility of its ways and modes must follow. Else he, she or it could as well be a Demonic clown who allows humans—innocent children—to be slain for sport)

Thus it follows, even from the most generic examples (presupposing a supernatural, omnipotent force) that human ethics trumps divine ethics on its face. If this is so, then it must also trump any and all human *extensions* of divine ethics, whether the ten commandments, canon law or wherever. Hence, it follows that human ethics and ethical standards can exist independently of invoking any divine or religious fluff, affiliations or baggage.

In terms of said "baggage" what the religionists have done is to take the natural code of (humane) ethics most people follow and embellish it with a blizzard of superstitious precepts and injunctions. These are superstitious since, inevitably, they are linked to the supposed dictates of a supernatural "being" that will not hesitate to "punish" those who disobey "him."

Ethics (or morality) without god is human behavior elevated to its highest consistent standards without the need for baffling with bullshit or, in this case, interjecting an external, non-physical but supreme moral arbiter where none is required.

3. Most criminals and insane are atheists

In a way, this is derivative from the preceding myth. After all, if one doesn't adhere to a God, it's possible s/he has no morals and may be criminal or insane because of it. I used to think this had only a small following until I accidentally got a glimpse of Tucker Carlson's MSNBC show[5], in which he presented survey statistics that disclosed a majority of physicians "believed in God." He acknowledged (to an atheist guest or at least someone playing Devil's Advocate) that this was a "good thing" since otherwise doctors might think they were gods.

---

5.   *The Situation*: aired on June 23, 2005 under the segment header "Doctors."

Leaving this foolishness out, since the existence of a single, uniform deity hasn't yet been proven or even minimally demonstrated, he then went on to assert it was a good thing for people in general to think someone was "looking down on them" since otherwise: Who knew what they would do?

I refer to this as the "Big Daddy in the Sky" motif, since it's predicated on an infinite version of Celestial "Homeland Security" where each human is tracked every second, every minute in every thing he or she does. It's also totally preposterous, apart from being insulting, debasing and childish. Certainly, from a rational point of view, anyone who avoids wrongdoing because of fear of being "caught by Cosmic Daddy" has a much more primitive and degenerate morality that an upstanding atheist who simply acts decently because he believes all humans merit respect and basic tolerance.

One can query why any God worth Its salt would accept such a loser into his "Heaven." I mean, this person isn't obeying out of *innate love of God*, but because s/he fears getting caught and ending up in the eternal barbecue pit! Is there a real case to be made here for the divine to embrace cynical, exploitative cowards?

But let's return to this "Homeland Security of God" racket. Despite Tucker Carlson's childish TV slot endorsement, it actually has had a long history in the Roman Catholic Church. That is, early on in Church history "sins of thought" were incorporated into the "mortal sin" transgression matrix. The architects of these "sins of thought" pointed to a biblical verse for validation, noting that even Christ said that a man who merely looked at a woman with lust in his heart had committed fornication, at least in *thought.*

From here it was but one step to introduce the ubiquitous "impure thoughts" as mortal sins in their own right, meaning that if one entertained them then died in a sudden accident his (or her) soul was as Hell bound as if actual illicit, premarital sex acts had transpired.

To reinforce this point, a former Franciscan priest named Emmett McLoughlin once cited statistics to show Catholics were more preponderant in mental hospitals than other religious populations.[6] He noted that "sins of thought" were at

---

6.   Emmett McLoughlin, 1962: "Let the Statistics Tell Their Tragic Story," in *Crime and Immorality in the Catholic Church*, Lyle Stuart Books, New York, pp. 189-214.

least partly to blame for this.[7] Thus, a Catholic teen that entertains "impure thoughts" knows he can as easily be earmarked for the eternal toaster as if he had actually committed fornication.

Consequently, as I can attest as a former Catholic, one spends a great deal of time monitoring all incoming thoughts. Is this one "impure"? If so, it must be abolished within about three nanoseconds, or one risks "grave sin." When does a minor impure thought become a major violation? According to one priest I asked while on a high school retreat: "When the image or woman has on less clothing than skin to cover!"

The beauty of "thought sins" is they open the gateway to perpetual mind control. As each thought registers it becomes the 800 lb. gorilla in the room (your mind). You try your best to ignore thinking of the latest Playmate in all her nude splendor, but she's sitting right there in your consciousness, so you can't. The more you try to avoid her, the more she returns, until you finally relent and give in to it. When you do, the attendant thought that *"God has recorded it"* instantly impinges. You must then run, not walk, to the nearest confessional! "Bless me, Father, my last Confession was five days ago. I just thought of that naked July Playmate again!"

As the cycle of thought betrayal and confession continues, one becomes more paranoid that in the next permutation he won't make it to confession in time and will end up as Satan's fodder. This leads to a persistent mental torment that afflicts all devout Catholic youths, sending them into precarious mental states and neurosis.

In my case, by the time I was twenty, I knew I had only two choices: reject Catholicism lock, stock and barrel, or end up in a psych ward someplace, on an hourly diet of thorazine. Probably strapped into a straightjacket as I beheld little demons flaying me with pitchforks awaiting my entry into Hell. I chose the atheist, full renunciation of faith escape route and never looked back. It also enabled me to experiment sexually, without the burden of shame or guilt.

Had I not escaped the mental straightjacket of "thought sins" I've no doubt I'd have remained a virgin at least until the age of 35, and perhaps much longer.

---

7.   *Op. cit.*, p. 177.

I'm also convinced my frustration levels would have metastasized to a critical breaking point, as well as mental instability driven by fear, shame and guilt. So, to me, leaving the Church was a matter of personal survival and one might even say "personal salvation."

The moral of the story that became clear to me over the years, especially during the period before I finally broke away completely, is that religiously induced insanity is vastly more probable than irreligiously induced. I haven't budged from that position since, despite some "research" that purports to show faith-grounded folks are paragons of health, and mental wellness. In point of fact, it's highly plausible most of these studies are based on bogus statistics, or at least selection effects that render the data nearly useless. What is evident is massive inconsistency between purported "happiness" and faith studies and often serial cancellations by other studies[8].

Do I think that atheists may sometimes be susceptible to more melancholy than their Christian cohorts? Possibly, and more because at the end of the day the atheist realizes and fully accepts that he's an orphan in a purposeless cosmos, and there are no cosmic Santas waiting to spirit him away to a better place after his final demise. Or to put a finer point on it, there is no hyper-dimensional Being ready and willing to take him into Its infinite, ethereal arms and hold him in a loving embrace. He's alone in the cosmos, and as a mature, intelligent and rational being he has to finally put away the things of a child.

Given that atheism is not for the faint-hearted or the mentally needy, it makes sense that sometimes atheists will feel their lack of cosmic connections to some pretend Higher Power more than believers. There's no mystery here! Nonetheless, most of the time atheists are in fine fettle because they know *they* create their own purpose.

4. Atheists Always Recant Near Death.

I confess that I haven't been able to address this for myself yet, mainly because I haven't come close to death. However, I would hope that if and when that fatal hour comes, I would hold firm to my principles and not simply cop out and

---

8.   See: Nathan Bupp, Humanism and the Science of Happiness, in *Free Inquiry*, October-November, 2006, Vol. 26, No. 6, p. 31.

squeal for the nearest priest to administer my insurance policy in the form of Extreme Unction because I feared some vague eternal fate.

Giving optimism on this score, are the deaths of two foremost American atheists: Isaac Asimov, and Carl Sagan. Neither capitulated to superstition in the final hour, though the prospect of death did bring further opportunity for reflection as it would for any sentient and intelligent being.

Nevertheless, those who embrace the traditional form of "Pascal's Wager," assume I am merely being an obstinate idiot. "*What have you got to lose?*" they ask. "If you *believe* you lose nothing in this wager. If you're wrong and there is no God after all, so what? All you forfeit is your pride. But if you don't believe, you stand to lose everything!"

Hence, they argue, the sane bet is to believe, rather than withhold belief.

I disagree. Let's consider it from two viewpoints: one of which assumes a real infinite (non-local) entity and one that doesn't. In the first case, and ironically, the most plausible basis for a real deity is that quantum non-locality governs consciousness. The result is a transpersonal and super-conscious state that precludes localized classes, or manipulations of such.

In this super consciousness, all times are immediately accessible, the past as easily as the future, because in hyper-dimensional consciousness all times are linked. This consciousness is not locked into a serial process of events that unfold one at a time. It "sees" everything at once. Ego-less, it's without a sense of personal identity or self in the sense of asserting power/status, occupying territory or projecting hegemony over nature. In addition, language and logic, with their built-in divisiveness are not comprehensible to this entity. The separation of subject from object, as well as logical categories, would be perceived as purely illusory artifacts.

Physicist Henry Margenau has compared reality perception for a finite being (such as a human) and a boundary-free being on the basis of "time slits".[9] In particular, he notes the latter would *lack a time slit* and this absence is precisely what

---

9.   Henry Margenau.: 1987, *The Miracle of Existence*, New Science Library, p. 121. Margenau's use of the term "time slit" is intended to represent the temporal analog of a spatial slit, e.g. what extent of a room is visible to you see if you observe it through a narrow "slit", say a keyhole?

makes all times instantly accessible. Humans, meanwhile, "are constrained by a narrow slit in the time dimension". This narrowness of temporal dimension creates our sense of isolation, along with our limited three-dimensional body and sense apparatus. This can be understood better by reference to the diagram below:

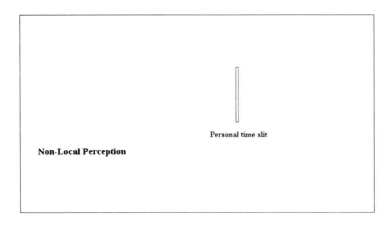

Figure. 5: Holistic and egocentric perceptions compared. Each human goes through life as if constrained to peer through a narrow slit which gives the impression of personal isolation. The holistic or non-local view is much vaster and hence appears to connect all entities within its field of perception.

The minds that we have, obviously, can only process within the limits of our time slits and the perceptions attendant on them. Thus, asked to envisage some eternal "punishments" compatible with our God-concepts we invariably arrive at those emphasizing isolation and separation first, and extreme punishment ("Hell"), second. Not surprisingly, when you ask the most serious orthodox Christians for their depictions of Hell, they respond: "a mental state of complete isolation from God's presence, leading to complete eternal anguish and loss". This, they indicate, is the real meaning and significance of Hell's "fires," since genuine fires can't be sustained over eternity.

The problem is that this limited time slit version of Hell, which is a human byproduct, doesn't square with the only genuine transpersonal or non-local entity that might pass as a God! Indeed, it contradicts it! What it does, essentially, is demand that the non-local, time-slit liberated version of deity revert to a narrow time-slit version of deity when applying punishment—presumably for those who eschew belief in it. The problem is that if it reverted to this time-slit version it would have to contradict its own nature!

One is led to conclude that the most reliable concept of a deity: a transpersonal entity with zero time constraints (consonant with an infinite, non-local nature) would be incapable of applying punishment to lesser beings in its firmament. The reason is that such punishment requires actions on the level of "isolation" or "separation" that are incompatible with non-locality. A Being that so acted, therefore, would be cognizant not only of its creatures' isolation but *its own*! Hence, recognize its own finitude and limits and could not therefore be omniscient or omnipresent!.

To make this more concrete, if such an entity (which is more or less analogous to Bohm's "Holomovement") existed, it would have to be literally blind to any transgressions against it, and certainly to puny human disbelief. This "blindness" arises not from overlooking human deficiency, but rather from its non-local nature that cannot at once be boundary-free and also localized in perceptions, to the extent of isolating a part of existence for "punishment". Consider the sketch below that shows the Holomovement depicted as "the ALL".

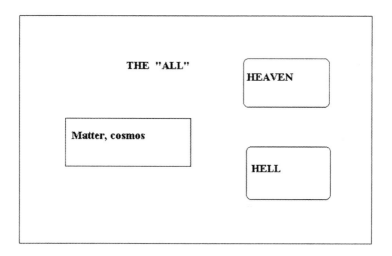

Figure. 6: A truly boundary-free consciousness with compartmentalized subsets within it. This is patterned after Bohm's Holomovement concept. In principle, such a non-local consciousness is incapable of consigning any of its elements to "Hell" or "Heaven" It would mean separating itself from itself: an impossibility.

In the end, if this entity existed (and I reiterate we've no evidence it does, only that the attributes are most consistent with the traditional "infinite, eternal" Being) then the atheist has nothing to fret over. At death, his limited temporal existence is simply subsumed into a greater, timeless existence. In effect, belief or no, he (like all the billions of other humans who've ever lived) must be integrated within the same boundary-free, non-local existence. The bottom line is that orthodox Christians simply can't have their "cake and eat it.". If they want unbelievers to suffer eternal torments, then they will have to part ways with an omnipresent, eternal deity!

Pascal's Wager for an atheist, based on such an entity, is a "gimme." But how can one be certain its vengeful, toting up snubs and sins counterpart doesn't exist? We can't, but there are many sound reasons for asserting that it doesn't, and that the vengeful deity is really simply a vengeful construct fabricated by limited human minds. Isolated and constricted minds that have projected their own ego needs, personal defects and need for vengeance and "justice" onto it. As we already saw, one reason is that an eternal entity would have to have an infinite temporal "slit" rendering it essentially blind to temporal events. Alas, finite human minds with their presumptions, biases and faculties can't deal with this.

Such limited and finite minds are bound to see concepts such as "justice" and "morality" in predefined, human terms. To these constricted minds, *an eye for an eye* sums up pretty well their entire theology. Besides, what fun would is it be to always act righteously, then finally get to Heaven and discover you're denied seeing unbelievers roasted over an eternal furnace and hearing their screams? Not much!

The rational atheist takes a more expansive view and declares that faced with the prospect of eternal "torment" (especially in the form of perpetual "loss") or keeping the company of a petty tyrant who'd burn any human for mere disbelief, the former is surely the better bet.

Michael Martin actually turns this choice on its head in arriving at an alternative view of Pascal's Wager, based on a negative deity he calls the "Perverse Master" which (he imagines) acts in consistent contradiction to the "just God" of orthodox Christians[10]. For example, rather than rewarding belief or faith in itself, especially if such belief is predicated on fear of torment, this entity punishes it for any supernatural being (including itself) while *rewarding disbelief* with eternal bliss. (Clearly this "PM" prefers not to have millions of "yes men" surrounding it, who've only espoused belief to save their sorry hides!)

In presenting a three-option truth table (based on probabilities, e.g. p1, p2 and p3) for the Wager, Martin is correct in observing that the problem with Pascal's original version is there are other variants that he didn't consider. None of those variants is ruled out *a priori* by Martin since, in the absence of irrefutable evidence for any one, all others have at least a finite probability. So it is with the "Perverse Master."

Martin's truth table ends up as a 3 x 3 matrix that carries within each 'cell' a choice resulting from the product of the individual probability and the consequence. The choices include: belief in the Perverse Master, belief in the traditional Judaeo-Christian God and belief in neither.

I find even this a bit too simplified. I also dislike the term "Perverse Master" as well as its logical foundation. Surely, any entity for which insincere belief amounted to a slight would also punish *sincere unbelief*. I therefore think a better term is "*Demiurge*," or a demi-god that actually recognizes human sin and won't hesitate to inflict its version of justice for sin[11]. Toward the task of constructing a more faithful Pascal-type truth table, let's refer to it as DG for Demiurgic God.

Next there is the Socinian deity, which is limited by never knowing more than the most advanced consciousness existing in the universe at one time. If limited in consciousness, the Socinian deity will also make errors. Physicist Freeman Dyson describes this entity almost like a child[12]:

"The main tenet of the Socinian heresy is that God is neither omniscient or omnipotent. He learns and grows as the universe unfolds".

---

10. Michael Martin: 1990: "The Wager Refuted," in: *Atheism: A Philosophical Justification*, Temple University Press, p. 232.
11. See, for example, Elaine Pagels' explanation in her book, *The Gnostic Gospels*, p. 37, wherein *demiurgos* is a lesser divine being who gives the law and metes out judgments to those who violate it. Obviously, *demiurgos* is a primitive god-concept for a preliterate people or culture.
12. Freeman Dyson: *Infinite in All Directions*, Harper & Row, p. 119.

Dyson adds that the beauty of adopting this construct is that it "leaves room at the top for diversity."[13] As this entity "grows to fill the universe" it becomes as much a "diversifier" as a unifying force[14]. Let's refer to this entity as SG. (It should not be confused with DG)

Next, we have the pantheistic and impersonal (but infinite-via-the-vacuum) entity proposed by David Bohm and others: the Holomovement, or perhaps "Universal Mind." This entity neither judges nor is separate from its creation, since it must be imbued within its very fabric (according to the implicate order holography principle, see Fig. 4). So call this HG.

Finally, there's the possibility of no deity existing at all, so NG. We can set up the table as follows:

REVISED BET OUTCOMES ON PASCAL'S WAGER

ACTION/DEITY	DG	SG	HG	NG
Disbelief	$-\infty \times p$	-p	-P	P/2
Belief	$\infty \times p$	p	P	-P/2
Don't Know	?	0	0	0

Here, DG is closest to Pascal's classical Christian version of God, and the options of SG (Socinus' God) or HG (Holomovement) mark novel entries. The reason for introducing the latter is that infinite power, omniscience etc. simply doesn't square with what's actually observed in the domain of Terra Firma. Each small "p" represents a low, finite probability. Each capital "P" represents a high finite probability. The designation "P/2" denotes somewhere in between, perhaps the 'median' of probabilities between p and P.

Now, if we regard the table globally, we see at a glance that the infinite utility and disutility (for DG) cancels out. In the same manner, the high and low probabilities (for SG and HG, respectively) cancel out, or essentially so. The (±) expectations for NG ("No God") reflect that a negative disutility with negative finite probability (- P/2) attaches to having a belief in no God. Meanwhile, (+ P/2) with positive utility and positive, finite probability is attached to disbelief or *withholding belief* in a deity. (For reasons that have already been discussed in this book,

---

13. Dyson, F.: *op. cit.*, p. 120.
14. *Ibid.*

e.g. that the theist is the one making the claim to add to the reality, the atheist merely passively responds by withholding investment of his intellectual resources)

When all is said and done, four positive expected values (including one infinity) cancel four negative ones (including one infinity), leaving only null expectation values or zeros. This not only refutes Pascal's traditional wager, but also the basis for a Wager belief in any other halfway credible deities!

From these expectation results we conclude the atheist is on very firm logical grounds for his disbelief, and making the traditional Pascal Wager is knuckle-headed and a waste of time. It merely discloses that the Christian's "mark" hasn't done his or her full set of homework!

Aside from the theoretical and logical analyses, one need only read various soldiers' journals and accounts (many of which have appeared in newspaper letters, or magazine articles) to see that there are, in fact, many atheists inhabiting foxholes! Probably as many or more also inhabit cancer wards (as the late astronomer Carl Sagan once did). Again, the myth that no atheist would dare do so really pivots on the orthodox Christian's own perception of what s/he would do! But truly, a Christian attempting to put himself in the deathbed atheist's place to decide on how he'd do the wager is preposterous, not to mention presumptuous. This is because it will always be skewed by the projections of the Christian's own fears on the choices!

Hence, this projection always resides at the basis of the myth that atheist always recant when death stalks!

5. Hitler was an Atheist.

This myth is intended to achieve exactly what it appears to do: slander atheism by association with the most monstrous human imaginable. If, therefore, Hitler can be painted as an "atheist" and if Hitler's deeds were so cumulatively vile, it follows (in a bizarre sort of logic) that atheism can only produce vile deeds. However, technically Hitler was a *Roman Catholic*. Robert Payne notes[15]:

---

15. Robert Payne: 1973, *The Life and Death of Adolf Hitler*, Praeger Publishers, p. 15

"Adolf Hitler's birth certificate records that he was born at six o'clock in the evening on April 20, 1889, and goes on to record that two days later, at a quarter past three in the afternoon, *in the presence of Father Ignaz Probst, the boy was baptized in the local Catholic Church*"

As is known from standard Roman Catholic doctrine, once one is baptized a Catholic, he or she technically remains a Catholic unless excommunicated, or until death. Payne later documents Catholic Church attendance by a number of Hitler's luminaries, including Gregor Strasser, Erich von Ludendorff and others.[16]

Ian Kershaw documents Hitler's regret and "*mistake in antagonizing the Catholic Church*"[17]. Primarily because Karl Lueger's Christian Socialist Party had made such a "deep impression on him"[18] given that it "was soldered together to appeal to Catholic piety and the economic self-interest of the German speaking lower middle classes."[19]

Both Payne and Kerhsaw also document the extensive fertile soil provided by the anti-Semitic *Völkisch* movement (which Hitler played to), by the German Catholic Church itself, i.e. in depictions of the Jews as "Christ Killers" such as in their Passion Play at Oberammagau etc.

While it is true that Hitler was probably no more than a nominal Catholic by the time of the invasion of Poland in 1939, this doesn't mean he was an "atheist" any more than the two Columbine killers (who professed being "atheists") as they threatened any peers that refused to budge from their faith during the 1999 Colorado killing spree. Obviously these killers merely *postured unbelief*, invoking the red-flag word "atheist", as a vehicle for their anti-social acts or to garner more media attention.

In fact, given Hitler's hatred of Communists (clearly and historically associated with atheism), it makes more sense that he would have grouped both in the same undesirable category. And, by that I mean earmarked them for "final solution." Let's also bear in mind that it was the Vatican that assisted Nazi war crimi-

---

16. *Op. cit.*, p. 386.
17. Ian Kershaw: 1998, *Hitler Hubris—1889-1936*, W.W. Norton & Company, p. 34
18. Ibid.
19. Ibid.

nals to escape Europe along the infamous "ratlines" to South America, just after World War II.[20]

Closer to the mark, but no less egregious, is the claim that "Stalin was an atheist" and hence we atheists ought to feel terrible because of Stalin's murderous reign. Again, the key point is missed. That is, conflating and confusing the deeds of voracious mass-murdering *individuals* (who manage to gain control of state machinery) with the coincidental philosophies they may claim to embrace at the time.

Let's also bear in mind that the Inquisition, for example, met with the blessings of actual popes who gave it their seal of approbation and essentially determined that it was consonant with the doctrines of the Church itself. (The rationale being to spare any heretics from the far worse fate of eternal torment!). Pope Innocent IV, for example, issued a famous (or infamous) Bull known as *Ad extirpanda*, which provided the machinery for systematic persecution as part of the state itself. This included seizure of property, possessions.[21]

This is at wide variance to Stalin et al, who merely seized the power of the state machinery available but invoked *NO godless doctrine per se* to rationalize it. It was merely his own paranoia and lust for consolidating power, combined with megalomania and bloodthirstiness. But no *doctrinal benediction* as was the case with the Inquisition!

6. Atheism is a Religion

This claim is absurd on its face. The misplaced strategy, however, is always to attempt to place atheism within the same logical context as religion and then attack it on the basis of occupying an analogous "belief" spectrum. In the end, this is a fool's errand.

For one thing it turns the very meaning and basis of religion on its head. We know all religions embody centralized beliefs or dogmas that issue from some sacred scripture or a body of theology based on scriptural interpretations. Athe-

---

20.   See: Mark Aarons and John Loftus, *Unholy Trinity: The Vatican, The Nazis and The Swiss Banks*, St. Martins Press, 1996, p. 288.

21.   Henry Charles Lea, *The Inquisition of the Middle Ages*, Barnes & Noble, 1954, p. 33.

ism has none of these, since there are no central propositions or beliefs with which all atheists agree.

First, atheists *withhold belief,* they do not invest it. This alone separates atheists from religionists or people of faith. Second, atheists make *no positive claims* for any transcendent existent that requires their worship or obeisance. They simply acknowledge no god or entity with which to build a religion in other words. Third, atheists maintain no sacred works, scriptures, or ancient artifacts, from which their "truths" are extracted.

They have no analog to a Bible, Qu'ran, Talmud or anything remotely similar. Instead, atheists pursue objective truth via open inquiry predicated on current science, which may provide fewer certainties or answers than if they merely placed their faith in a book.

Fourth, atheists convene no regular rituals, services or ceremonies to honor, or propitiate any entity. By contrast, the centerpiece of 99 percent of religions is precisely some social ritual, for the purpose of assembling together like-minded *believers* toward a common goal. Moreover, their churches, synagogues, temples etc. dot the landscape, taking up room that could be used to house the homeless in each respective area or locale.

Perhaps most importantly, there is no "acceptance" of atheist principles from any "congregation" since there's no homogeneous congregation to bestow it. Atheists often disagree on as many things as they agree on, precisely because no formal coda exists to fix beliefs within a uniform dogma. This means one is just as likely to encounter a wholly Materialist-Naturalist atheist as a non-material one.

Despite this, there remain some who insist that if an atheist simply "doesn't believe in the supernatural or God" he is expressing a *belief.* If expressing a belief, then he is professing a *religion.* This is nonsense. It would be akin to asserting that if I decline belief in UFOs as extraterrestrial spacecraft I still have "UFO belief" and therefore am a practicing Ufologist! The error inheres in asserting that an *absence of belief* is the same as a belief. This error repeats the canard that the onus is on the atheist to disprove the believer's claim, instead of acknowledging it is impossible to prove a negative[22].

Our goal, based on reason and the most current scientific findings, is to secure a niche in society for ourselves, mostly for the ideas that society itself dismisses, and for our own mutual *self-acceptance*.

7. All Atheists are Materialists

As well as being an atheist, I'm a Materialist and proud of it.

Materialism as a working philosophy embraces both large-scale cosmic inter-actions and atomic scale or quantum phenomena. The latter are not necessarily "material," i.e., quantum interference patterns, but they are *physical*. Hence Materialism as it is understood today embraces all physical fields and interactions, of both matter *and* energy. The laws governing these interactions apply without exception to humans as well as inanimate particles/objects. The prediction of the future behavior of all physical interactions is not dependent on the existence of any supernatural agency. Thus, physical laws are complete in the sense of being able to account for all physical phenomena.

As a philosophy of life, Materialism places a premium on objective truth arrived at from the available evidence, accessible to all rather than dispensed on high from Councils, dogmas, "sacred" texts or papal encyclicals. If the ecclesiastic supernaturalist can be deprived of a *raison d'etre* then dignity and intellectual integrity can be authentically restored to Man. Value and worth is transferred from some hereafter to the here and now; and the power currently vested in Church hierarchies is conveyed to Man himself.

Not surprisingly, the Materialist is more likely than the supernaturalist to place a premium on revering the Earth and demanding the rational disposition of its resources. As a Materialist, after all, I can examine the existing evidence and determine that our planet is probably the only inhabited one in the Milky Way. I can also ascertain that this life is most likely the only one and that I must strive to

---

22. Some sophists attempt to get around this by claming *it isn't impossible* to prove a neg-ative. They argue that they can prove "there are *no* black balls" in a box by simply emptying the box out and finding all white balls. But this misrepresents the example, since the possibility of "all white" balls was never in question! The analogy is specious because the existence of God IS in question, and *isn't objectively verifiable* like count-ing real balls. The analogy trivializes the deity existence question while not validating the sophist.

enhance it in any way possible. I should emphatically not squander what I have now, while awaiting a mythical afterlife.

As a Materialist I therefore refrain from looking to any hypothesized deity for deliverance, or lay blame for human ills on some mythical demonic entity. On the contrary, Man alone is responsible for his actions and is the ultimate master of his fate. As a Materialist I maintain that Man need not suffer extinction as a species, if he has the courage and vision to assume control of his destiny through the use of reason.

It's not necessary to wave a Bible or the ten commandments at a Materialist, or even quote the "golden rule." The true Materialist, by definition, respects his fellow men and reveres all life, since he recognizes (through his philosophy) that they share one planet which may well be unique in the cosmos. Thus, the true Materialist treasures and conserves the Earth's finite store of resources, since he comprehends that Earth also has one life to live—and there is no more after the existing resources are consumed.

Embodied within the above is a practical ethics, forged out of the Materialist's reason and his priorities. The Materialist is compelled to co-operate with his fellows and promote a common good, not out of fear for the wrath of a deity, but to insure a thriving, harmonious community with high survival value.

Having said all that, it's not true that all atheists are necessarily Materialists. For example, while a member (briefly!) of Mensa's ATHSig, I found atheists who also professed belief in non-physical or non-material phenomena. At least one espoused that supernatural phenomena might exist and science ought to be open to such investigation.

While these are surely non-standard positions, they do mean that one cannot generalize about atheists. Even Sir A.J. Ayer, among the foremost atheists of his time, once professed his allowance that life after death might exist (after his own near death experience reported in an article in *The London Sunday Times* in 1988) though he did add that *"just as there can be a godless life, there can be a godless after life."*

However, any such afterlife is difficult to portray and describe (far less explain) in terms of a Materialist point of view. One would almost surely have to invoke esoteric quantum or sub-quantum concepts such as *de Broglie waves*, or the Bohmian quantum potential[23]. Most scientists, who share a Materialist outlook, are highly averse to even speculating in this way.

Many take what is called a "logical positivist" stance, that it's perfectly fine to ignore any and all interpretations of nature until hard evidence is forthcoming. We just pay attention to observables and measurements, nothing more.

Summary points:

1. Atheists can't deny God, since one cannot deny that which hasn't been shown to exist in the first place. (What sane person "denies" unicorns, elves and fairies?)

2. Atheists eschew Bible-based "morals" in favor of godless ethics, which is far more consistent and powerful in terms of inducing decent human behavior.

3. Most criminals and insane are religious not atheists, since most of the general population are religious. Atheists are under-represented in the prison and asylum populations, meaning that (as a percentage of the incarcerated population) there are far fewer atheists than Roman Catholics, Protestants, Jews or Muslims.

4. Atheists never recant at death since death is merely nature's means to advance evolution. When one dies, he or she is gone forever. So there is nothing to fear. The Heaven-Hell doctrine itself was introduced more than 300 years after the death of St. Peter, because the original teaching (*reincarnation*, as propounded by the Church Fathers Clement of Alexandria and Origen of Adamantius) was believed to "give Man too much time to seek God". Far better to have one ferocious and vile doctrine to frighten procrastinators into the fold by the end of one lifetime!

5. Hitler was a Roman Catholic, not an atheist. Christians who resort to the "Hitler was an atheist" argument demonstrate their ignorance of the fact that once one is baptized a Catholic one remains so, until or unless formally excommunicated.

---

23. David Bohm, "Preliminary Interpretation of Quantum Theory in Terms of Hidden Variables" in *Wholeness and the Implicate Order*, Routledge & Kegan-Paul, pp. 76-77.

6. Atheism cannot be a religion since there's no central dogma or sacred book around which to erect any consistent belief system. Nor do atheists pray or have any recognizable rituals to propitiate anything, including the plain ordinary physical cosmos. Nor do atheists have churches!

7. Atheism is broad and diverse, and not all atheists are Materialists. Indeed, Materialism itself has many branches and offshoots, including (but not limited to):

    - Physicalist Materialism (everything in the cosmos has a physical nature)

    - Epiphenomenalist Materialism (non-physical processes occur that are contingent on physical origins, organs, etc.)

    - Panpsychic Materialism (attributes a mental character to physical entities)

    - Emergent Materialism (can attribute vitalist forces to physical nature)

    - Dialectical Materialists (mental processes evolve from physical ones)

In this book, physicalist Materialism or physicalism is always assumed from the outset. "Materialism" is taken to mean *physicalist Materialism*, to retain continuity with ancient Materialism as a recognized philosophy. "Naturalism" has been proposed by some authors such as Paul Kurtz[24], but is eschewed in this book as being too ambiguous, value-neutral and apt to be confused or conflated with "naturalists" working in field ecology or biological science.

---

24. Paul Kurtz: "'Yes' to Naturalism, Secularism and Humanism", in *Free Inquiry*, April/ May 2007, p. 4.

3

Logical Fallacies Used on Atheists

Perhaps the most onerous burden shared by atheists is having to argue or debate people with minimal skills in logic or critical thinking. The first means that we can expect all manner of logical fallacies, flaws, and bogus arguments to be hurled our way. The second means that, rather than a genuine effort at uncovering truth, most of our detractors or critics are invested in promoting their own ideology at our expense. Ask them to consider one single fact, within a logical context, and watch them erupt.

It follows that the atheist can do no better than to stock his armament with all the logical, critical thinking strategies available. The more this is done, the greater the likelihood of fending off attacks. In today's hostile climate of increasing Christian evangelical hegemony, this can spell the difference between survival and being totally marginalized and rendered a scapegoat.

What I'd like to do is examine each of the main logical fallacies in turn, including examples of how they might be used against an atheist and ways to respond to each. None of this is intended to be complete, or self-sufficient, since there are alredy a number of excellent books available to help people to navigate the waters of logic and critical thinking.

1. Ignotum per Ignotius

Of all the fallacies, I think this is the most endemic and pervasive within the U.S. cultural war landscape. This dates from as far back as 1925, when Christian "design" model creationists argued the best "cure for atheism" was the structure and design of the eye. Well, hardly! Since, after all, the eye "sees" optimally at a particular wavelength (~ 5500 Å) of light, precisely because it evolved on a planet with a star whose maximum radiation output is *at that wavelength*!

What is the logical fallacy of *ignotum per ignotius*? Basically it translates from the Latin to mean: "seeking to explain the not understood by the less well understood." In this case, attempting to account for the alleged grandiose "design" of the human eye by appeal to totally unknown constructs (e.g. a supernatural or unknown "designer"). This, after all, would have to be the subtext if the eye's design is being viewed as "a cure for atheism". (E.g. the atheist is compelled to surrender evolution via natural selection, since the inherent randomness cannot account for the splendid design).

The problem with this line of argument is that it invokes a less well-known or understood mechanism ("the designer") to account for a structure or organ whose origin may not be fully apprehended at this moment. But *who* or what is this designer? The proponents of the various forms of creationism (including the now fashionable intelligent design) won't say, but it doesn't require an Einstein to infer they are interjecting a supernatural agent. That is, "God."

The problem is that all intelligent design (ID) has done is to subsume naturalistic evolution's observations then magically assert they are produced by "intelligent design", since no random process could possibly arrive at such intricacy in a billion years. Thus, rather than accept a fairly well understood random process ID'ers opt to nix it in favor of a much less well understood "designer" about whose specifics, attributes they are totally silent.

All they can offer up is the canard that: "X, Y or Z structures display irreducible complexity," hence there must be some unseen intellect working behind the scene to create it! This is pure nonsense as well as a circular argument.

On a recent trip to Alaska, my wife and I traveled to just below the Arctic Circle to watch the aurora. We clambered out of a snow-cat to stay with a group of other visitors high on a hillside, from near midnight to two in the morning. As we watched the sky above, occasionally repairing to a yurt to keep warm, we beheld the most majestic and intricate sights.

Above us, enormous, parallel green tubes lined up and stretched from one horizon to the other. My wife exclaimed as she looked on in fascination: "Gosh! They look like giant, artificial fluorescent tubes in the sky!"

I agreed. They also appeared far too artificial and intricate to be the product of random processes, but they were. As every beginning student in space plasma physics knows, order can appear at any time in complex plasma systems. For the spectacle we beheld, the procession to order was dictated by the (pre-existing) presence of the auroral oval around the North pole and the polar electro-jet. In tandem these made up a kind of pre-prepared stage or setting.

The other "actor" in place was none other than the Earth's planetary magnetic field. Now, add a blast of impinging electrons from the solar wind and *Voila*! You have the basis for the creation of giant parallel tubes of green light across the sky! In this case, the incoming electrons decelerate into the pre-existing oval and form currents in sheets. These are then shaped, and "rolled" by the ambient magnetic field of Earth. Fluctuations of the field in tandem with the variable density of incoming electrons, and the altitude at which atmospheric atoms lose their electrons, engender all sorts of wonders.

At places like the University of Alaska-Fairbanks, space physicists have been able to devise numerical simulations of the aurora using sophisticated computer programs. Not only can they duplicate many types of auroral displays but one can see the emergence of a definite order from a chaotic plasma background. The aurora forms from plasma sheets and currents in the high ionosphere and many chaotic processes underpin this formation. What we have, to use the words of Ilya Prigogine (from the title of one of his books) is "Order out of Chaos."

What does all this mean? Simply that the temptation to put the cart before the horse and invoke "designers" for every intricate shape or natural structure is unwarranted. It also does a gross disservice to human intelligence, since the implicit assumption is that human brainpower is perpetually ill-suited to ever discover the underlying processes behind nature's most awesome shapes.

To paraphrase the philosopher David Hume[1]:

> "No testimony is sufficient to establish a miracle, unless the testimony be of such a kind that its falsehood would be more miraculous than the fact which it endeavors to establish."

---

1.   David Hume: *An Enquiry Concerning Human Understanding*, Sec. X "Of Miracles", Prometheus Books, 1988, p. 103.

This can also be applied to intelligent design merely by replacing the word "miracle" with "designer". It affords, then, an excellent rule of thumb by which to disqualify fallacies of the ignotum per ignotius variety.

For example, consider the example of the eye again. Is the *falsehood* of its intelligent design more miraculous than the fact it attempts to establish that the eye is the product of intelligent design? Arguably no. While the falsehood would leave random chance as a primary agent, random chance in no way is "more miraculous" or incredible than the initial ID proposal!

The central problem of ID, is that though its muddled adherents make multiple fusses about some particulars to do with evolution's evidence, they *never* come up with ID's presumed *unique evidence* to support its claimed "irreducible complexity". Any time they do, the real scientist can show a process whereby the same structure or organism can be better explained by a combination of natural selection, adaptation *over time*.

A much more sophisticated species of *ignotum per ignotius* can be found in the premise and use of "intuitive physics" such as discussed by Pascal Boyer.[2] Here, Boyer discusses how ordinary people parse and interpret reality according to "inference systems" based in the brain. All of these are evidently predicated on some kind of physical intuition by which the brain concludes certain types of causation, as well as expectations of what objects in discrete mental categories can and cannot do. This in turn affects how one sorts these objects in one's experience, and more exactly making ontological distinctions between them.

The end point is that religious experience, because it can contradict expected categories and ontological distinctions, belongs in a class by itself and cannot be judged solely on scientific criteria. Supernatural concepts, then, are possible once they allow a "violation of expectations". So if I assert an all-seeing Being follows our every action and monitors us 24/7 but is powerless to stop hurricanes like Katrina (or chooses not to in order to permit us exercise of "free will") I am not being ironic, or facetious.

---

2.   Pascal Boyer: 2001, *Religion Explained: The Evolutionary Origins of Religious Thought*, Basic Books, Chapter 3, "The Kind of Mind It Takes."

Of course, this isn't so and in every investigation worth its salt, empirical observations and established scientific principles (as well as causality) always trump "intuitive" perceptions. In modern terms, science allows what we call a "disjunctive plurality of causes" (e.g. multiple causes for one event or outcome) as well as indeterminate causality which is expected from quantum mechanics.

Consider quantum causality as an aside. Because quantum mechanics opened up an entirely new field of logic (known as quantum logic), new rules and postulates arose for which the logical classical definitions are inadequate. In classical logic, for example, one can say that either an electron will go through slit A in an interference experiment, OR slit B. Under no circumstances can there be an expectation where the electron goes through both slits. Yet in many versions of the typical electron diffraction experiment this is just what occurs!

The point is that, contrary to the impressions of many, modern science is rich enough to encompass all manner of claimed phenomena and interpret these in an objective light without appeal to supernatural explanations or some inferential solipsism.

2. Red Herring.

In any argument or debate with a religionist, the most anticipated tactic is always the red herring. This tried and true ruse represents an effort to re-direct a debate away from its central issue to a marginal or peripheral one.

Example:

"Look at all the crime, the murders and the drugs going on! If it weren't for atheists we'd have none of these!"

In fact, none of the above are related to atheism. No one has demonstrated, certainly to any degree of competence, even the most cursory correlation between atheism and general crime stats, murder specifically, or drugs. In all likelihood then, they arise from deep societal pathologies, or from lack of social-psychological services, including addiction treatment centers.

However, in the mind of the religious, the atheist is a convenient scapegoat because of his seeming "amorality". As the embodiment of godlessness, therefore, he is depicted as the weakest link in the chain of social order. Remove the weakest link, and Voila! Society morphs into what it should be: a lawful, decent and orderly structure.

This sort of red herring, while egregious in its own right, also forces the demonization of atheists. We are to be identified as walking, talking moral scourges who inflict a tendency to evil-doing on any vulnerable person in the society

Example from an online 1994 debate about the Rwanda genocide and why God chose not to intervene to save lives.

> "What can YOU say *for atheism*? Why didn't your great atheism prevent these Rwandan atrocities?"

This is a subtler red herring, since it tries to turn the tables on the atheist by making his non-belief equally accountable as the omnipotent Christian God. But, in truth, the atheist can't be accountable or responsible for "preventing genocide" since he's not the one admitting to worship of or claiming existence for an *infinite, all-powerful, all-knowing Being*! A Being, given its resume, that ought to be able to do anything, help any innocent anywhere, and then some.

The correct response for the Christian, therefore, is not to impugn atheism for its alleged impotence in preventing genocide, but to admit that s/he doesn't know why God (as an all-powerful, infinite Being) *chose not to intervene*. Such specious reasons as "it is not up to humans to fathom the Divine" have been offered from time immemorial, so why not in this instance? Perhaps because the respondent believes (rightly) that it's hackneyed and trite and might be treated with disdain. But this foresight can't be used as a justification for a blatant red herring.

Remember again, the most basic form of atheism (the implicit or "weak" form) is the *withholding of belief.* There is no positive investment in any special, divine entity so there's no acknowledgement of anything other than a randomly contrived, purposeless cosmos. Humans can't expect divine intervention into tribal or social aggression, any more than we can expect it into a natural disaster like a tsunami.

Humans inhabit a gigantic, spherical "pinball" machine in which random chance dominates outcome, not any "god" or "divine will". At any instant any naturally induced calamity can occur, whether hurricane, tsunami or earthquake, and wipe out a mass of humanity. Who gets nailed is totally a matter of the "luck of the draw" at the time, nothing more or less. If, however, a divine being of infinite and all-powerful attributes *did exist*, the very least we could expect is passive intervention into natural disasters. (E.g. allowing a tornado or other disaster to strike an uninhabited region). This is irrespective of whether it declined to meddle in human "evil" on the basis of some misguided notion of "free will".

Example from another online debate:

"I believe in God, YOU believe only in empiricism!"

This is a red herring as well as false analogy since empiricism hasn't a thing to do with the issue of belief or non-belief. Empiricism is *a scientific process* that predicates the approach to objective truth on empirical data that later may become empirical facts. There is nothing to believe! You either apply empirical tests, as a bona fide scientist, or you don't (if you're into metaphysics).

For example, in observing the Sun over a period of months or years, one can accumulate data on: changing sunspot area, occurrence of specific types of solar flares (e.g. different optical and morphological classes). When this data is assembled into categories (e.g. A for sunspot area, F for flare frequency etc.), and fitted statistically, it can describe a rudimentary empirical system or ansatz.

If I do a linear regression to find a fit for F (flare frequency, or flares per day) vs. A(area) of a sunspot group, I may obtain a statistical function of the form:

$$F = A(S1) + C$$

where C is some quantity that intersects the particular (y-axis), in this case the one for F.

This is a mathematical representation of an empirical relationship. The mathematical form is dictated by how the data fits, and is a matter of using standard statistical tests. The empirical system that results is not a matter of "belief" but simply the degree of goodness of fit for the data. An example graph from a study I did of just such data is shown below:

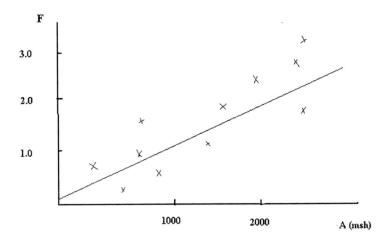

Figure. 7: Plot of flare frequency vs. sunspot area in msh or millionths of a solar hemisphere.

In acquiring the data via random sample, and then assembling it as shown in Fig. 7, a precise mathematical procedure was used, resulting in what is called a "least squares regression" line. This represents the best fit given the data points. Thus, if one uses such a relationship to assert that flare frequency increases with the associated sunspot group area, this is not a matter of "belief" but hard, empirical science.

Supporting that is the image below of a large sunspot group photographed in November, 1980. It was found that the larger area group generated more flares than the smaller one.

Figure 8. Large and small area sunspot groups used to generate the
graph in Fig. 7

However, in their red herrings, religionists like to expand their rhetoric and invoke such procedures as a basis for a "counterpart" deity, where in fact none exists. Sadly, explaining all this will never stop the faithful from using such tactics, though one might at least ask them for a graph showing the linear regression of their "design" say, on the number of components in the human eye.

3. Arguing from authority.

If you've ever argued with orthodox Christians, how often have you heard them cite chapter and verse from their Bible? The tendency has become so predictable it resembles a kind of Pavlovian reflex. You start a rational argument with a believer, and within five minutes he's trotting out the old canard:

"The fool hath said within his heart there is no God!"

If that citation doesn't work, look for him to go back to his biblical or scriptural grab bag for some other forlorn, antiquated quote, all in an effort to convince you that *you,* Mr. or Ms. Heathen, are going against two thousand year old authority and God's holy writ! The favorite quotes, by the way, seem to be all those dealing with "Hell" in the New Testament, or related to the end times and the "Beast" written about in Revelation. All of these, as well as the psychotic personality portrayed in the Old Testament, disclose concepts fashioned by human minds. Martin Foreman hits the nail squarely on the head when he writes[3]:

"No self-respecting human author, far less an all-knowing deity, would suggest (the Bible) is worthy to be considered a holy text"

Catholics at least are somewhat less predictable than Protestants, maybe because Catholics were forbidden to read the Bible for centuries, so didn't develop the incredible dependence displayed by many evangelical Protestants. No, the Catholics will be sure to toss in various Canon laws, as well as citations from papal encyclicals like *Humanae Vitae.*

In all these cases the argument is from authority, whether based on a papal note or an ancient epistle. What I like to do is ask my opponent to drop his or her book and simply argue from straight reason, starting with providing a rational answer to the question:

Why is your faith credible, apart from the existence of any "sacred" texts or personal anecdotes?

Most are unable to do that, at least for any sustained time.

4. Begging the Question.

Of course unbelievers are going to Hell! Christ said so himself in the Bible!

Of course unbelievers are going to Hell! Why should righteous Christians have to share heaven with them!

Of course unbelievers are going to Hell! You think you will find Hitler in Heaven?

Of course unbelievers are going to Hell! If they don't believe in him, why would God want them?

Of course unbelievers are going to Hell! Where ELSE is there for Atheists to go after death?

---

3.   Martin Foreman, "Good News for Atheists—The Bible is NOT the word of God," reprinted in *Freethought Springs,* March, 2007 from the series by M. Foreman: *If God Existed, He Would be an Atheist.*

The above examples illustrate what is known as "begging the question". Arguing for the validity of a claim, in this case *unbelievers are going to Hell,* simply by repeating it over and over again in different words. Thus, this tactic is always recognized as somewhat like a broken record. It doesn't matter what the particular argument or claim is, it's the repetition that's the key. The verbal window dressing changes, but the essential core remains as hollow as the original.

The claim is tossed out, but there is never any follow up in the form of deductions, facts or conclusions, only the same tired refrain. Usually, when I'm confronted by this tactic, the claimant saying that X is so because of Y, W, Z and so on, I simply ask:

Well, which *one* of those is the basis for your argument?

Often, and incredibly, the response is "All", or "All of the above." which allows me to further respond:

> "Fine, then how about proving that EACH one of those is a valid proposition, then showing me how they each validate your claim".

In general, they suddenly acquire a "deer in the headlights" look and act shellshocked. When the eyes disclose the lights are on but nobody's home, it is time to recognize that they haven't a clue how to convert their question begging into a solid argument. By this time, the usual rejoinder after some minutes is to find an excuse to leave and go home.

5. Slippery Slope

Those who invoke slippery slope arguments want to convince you that cultivating atheism, or having an unbelief mindset, will launch the most stupendous catastrophes in the history of humanity or the cosmos. Biblical plagues of locusts, diseases, famines … not to mention terrorist attacks, will rain down on one and all. Families will be torn asunder. Homosexuality will reach new heights, since ethics or morals will be "neutralized." Abortions will be performed on a whim, since parents will feel (under an amoral atheist value system) that it's okay to off the fetus if the odds appear to show s/he won't be a future Pamela Anderson or Einstein.

Porn and sex predators will metastasize like cancer everywhere with nothing to stop them, not even the most exacting civil or federal laws. The fragile minds of the young will be contaminated non-stop until they won't be able to function at all, as the whole populace ultimately becomes porn "addicted".

The base thread in all slippery slope arguments is the assumption, or perhaps more accurately *the false assumption*, that some despised outlook or behavior will lead inexorably to a vastly worse outlook or behavior.

Although these tactics are insipid on their face, since no concrete evidence is ever presented to support them (or if it is, it's specious), they're invoked because people can be so easily misled. All that's required is a preconceived negative image (and the atheist has this in abundance) and the recipient of the disinformation will be ready to accept just about any claim.

Thus, when the birth control pill first became widely available, one heard a hue and a cry raised that it would mean "the end of the human race," since population would crash everywhere. Obviously, kids were high-maintenance beings and sucked the life out of most parents, so it followed most parents would now take the easy way out if provided the option. But, you know what? It didn't happen! Though millions bought the slippery slope that it might. (The Catholic Church, especially, which is why the encyclical *Human Vitae* was issued in 1968, albeit in opposition to Pope Paul IV's own papal commission!)

In fact, since the pill came out in the late 50s-early 60s the human population has nearly doubled. Prompting more than a few of us to wonder what might have transpired if the pill hadn't reached mass markets.

When the state of Alaska first passed its limited marijuana use law in the 80s, allowing small amounts for personal use, slippery slope again had been bandied about beforehand. *"The whole population will now go on to the harder stuff-crack. heroin, you name it!"*

A holiday visit by my wife and myself to Fairbanks and Anchorage in March, 2005, however, confirmed that industry, pride and productivity still formed the core of Alaskans' character. We saw it from the people who worked the float planes, to the hotel staff to the waiters, waitresses in the restaurants. None of these showed any signs of deleterious behavior or la-la land passivity induced by drugs.

Perhaps the most infamous slippery slope argument of all was invoked to delay or prevent the U.S. departure from a losing effort Viet Nam. It was based on the egregious "domino" theory, which became as entrenched and accepted among military bureaucrats, and think tank wonks as biblical inerrancy is among many evangelicals.

"Oh, we can't leave, not now! Not at this time! If we just pull out Viet Nam will be the first of many dominoes to fall across Southeast Asia! Next will be Cambodia, then Thailand (Myanmar), then Laos, then Malaysia and who knows where it will end? The Philippines too?"

As in the case of the (earlier) anticipated collapse of human numbers from artificial birth control and the feared conversion of most Alaskans to destitute druggies, it never happened. What did happen is the U.S. was forced to bail out in 1975, with over 58,000 American dead by that time. Whereas, the numbers would have been much less had fewer powerful minds not succumbed to the slippery slope "domino theory" nonsense.

Similar nonsense arguments are currently enlisted to try to prevent the U.S. from leaving another military quagmire in Iraq. (Though to be sure, the cost in casualties is more by way of slow attrition than outright large battles like in 'Nam). This time, the slippery slope is that if the U.S. leaves, the entire Middle East will fall to terrorists. And after that, they will follow us home and attack us in our Malls. Now, since we can't have that, it follows that we will have to stay in Iraq for generations! Problem is, where's the money going to come from (in a political landscape rife with tax cuts) to pay for it?

History shows, time and time again, that appeals to slippery slope reasoning often do much more harm to innocent people than they do to advance a case for some agenda, far less win any rigorous arguments with atheists.

6. Rigid Either—Or Reasoning.

Just as slippery slope tactics work because humans have the uncanny ability to extrapolate negativity and dire consequences beyond the support of the facts at hand, so does rigid either-or reasoning work because most human are conditioned to binary responses. Yes-no, 1 or 0, either this or that. Of course, the "Crossfire" syndrome, which cultivates only two sides in some attack format, prospers for this reason.

You have one side, call it A, versus another side, call it B. These sides, A and B, are assumed from the outset to be the only two available for discussion. This may be correct if one is confined to a "sound bite" format wherein time is at a premium, and opinions can't be fully analyzed.

In the real world, this is seldom the case. For example, there may be only one side that carries any validity. Thus, the Holocaust was real and actually occurred. There are not "two sides" to the issue and either-or reasoning about it is inapplicable. Global warming also has a scientific consensus and hard evidence to support it, so it isn't a case of "either global warming is occurring" or "global warming isn't occurring". It is, full stop.

At the same time, there *might be* issues that do have multiple positions. For example, in between the extreme positions that the U.S. must remain in Iraq come hell or high water, or abandon it immediately, there is the third or mean position of *a phased withdrawal.* This is done over a defined length of time, say two years.

In the case of the abortion debate, there are also nuanced positions between the two extremes of absolutely no abortion ever at any time, and abortion on demand. Thus, one may hold to abortion only in the first trimester, as was the Catholic Church's original teaching, until 1869. Or, one may modify this too by limiting it to the first trimester and only in cases of rape or incest.

Even the case of unbelief is not as open and closed an issue as it appears. For example, there are some who profess unbelief for any personal God, but yet embrace a wholly *impersonal one,* say based on energy. Such people can't technically be called atheists. Einstein, in this light, always professed belief in "Spinoza's God" which he identified with the inherent harmony of the cosmos as demonstrated in various natural laws and mathematical regularity.

George Smith[4] notes that the most vernacular usage confuses the meaning of *agnostic,* usually asserting it is "somewhere between belief and outright unbelief."

The way it is usually framed is that the agnostic "isn't sure whether or not God exists." In fact this is an erroneous interpretation of the term.

What it actually, technically means is someone who asserts *there is not yet adequate evidence to make a decision if one were possible.* In other words, the issue must remain open-ended and unresolved until such time evidence appears. Thus, true agnosticism is not some dithering or fence-sitting between belief and unbelief, but rather acknowledgement of *the impossibility of knowledge* as it pertains to any ability to address the question in the first place.

Smith himself (page 9) splits and parses the agnostic position even further, according to whether one is an *agnostic atheist* or an *agnostic theist.* The first avers that all supernaturalist propositions or claims are inherently unknowable (because they are untestable) by the human mind, and so not worth discussing any more than pink elves, unicorns or fairies. In this sense, unbelief isn't really even necessary, since who would actually believe in a pink elf or unicorn? Well, then there'd be even less merit to arguing over an invisible Being! Thus, without any capacity for knowledge about it, it's redundant.

The theist agnostic meanwhile, maintains a firm belief in the existence of God. But asserts the precise nature of this God is unknowable. On this basis, no attributes are assigned to try to define God's nature. We cannot say that any divine nature is "eternal", or "omnipotent" or "omnipresent" because one simply doesn't know. Thus, it makes no sense to use words to try to describe a deity. Belief is as far as one can go.

In his superb 1923 essay *Ich und Du* (I and Thou), Martin Buber put his finger on the inherent flaw of all binary thinking.

> *Men prefer to forget how many possibilities are open to them. They like to be told that there are two worlds and two ways. This is comforting because it is so tidy. Almost always one way turns out to be common and the other one is celebrated as superior.*

In the same essay, Buber goes on to show how this binary constraint on thought lends itself to a destructive 'Us against Them' dynamic. This makes possible a simple division of humans into two groups: "sheep and goats." One

---

4.   George Smith, *Atheism—The Case Against God,* 1989, Prometheus Books, p. 9.

blessed and imbued with all positive attributes: selflessness, courage, nobility, honor, decency etc. and the other "damned" and imbued with all the most vile attributes a human can possibly possess.

It isn't difficult to predict on which side the avowed atheist falls, if he or she is constrained to a binary debate. Indeed, just argue for a few minutes with any devout and orthodox Christian, and I promise you'll be propositioned along salvation lines. And there's almost no greater insidious insult than this obnoxious and arrogant position since it assumes all atheists, as "goats", are ipso facto bound for the eternal microwave unless salvaged by your nearest friendly Christian do-gooder[5].

Buddhist philosopher Alan Watts in his magnificent monograph, *The Wisdom of Insecurity*, noted that the path for peace on Earth is paved by cultivation of benign passivity as opposed to neurotic and paranoid ostracization and demonization of the "other". In achieving this, the attitude of "live and let live" is cultivated, and not changed unless one is directly attacked. One never acts merely upon speculations or even "possible threats". As Watts notes[6]:

> For all the qualities which we admire or loathe in the world around us are reflections from within … Our feelings about the crawling world of the wasps' nests and the snake pit are feelings about hidden aspects of our own bodies and brains

In other words, the aversion to the (metaphorical) "snakes" and "wasps' nests" of the world (identical say to 'atheists' or some other out group that embodies the 'demon' of the moment) is a reflection to an aversion existing within ourselves. Perhaps, just perhaps, the atheist arouses our fear and ire because, left to our own devices with no authorities or outside influences to manipulate us, we might choose that path too! Rather than acknowledge that unpleasant awareness, many

---

5.   Of course, the atheist side is not free from the "Us vs. Them" syndrome. But it's generally originated in response to Christian vitriol and arrogance rather than determined *ab initio*. As an aside, it matters not that such realms as 'Heaven', 'Hell', etc. don't exist *to me*, but that belief in them is the true insult, delivered by a venomous, insane and ignorant mentality. So let no proselytizing Christian Hell-believer come back with any bilge that "my beliefs ought not bother you since you don't believe in them!" They do! And further, they energize *my own rage and hatred against you*! Thus do we find much unnecessary Christian bashing in many atheist enclaves, groups.

6.   Alan Watts, *The Wisdom of Insecurity*, p. 111.

choose to paint the atheist as an aberration or even abomination. Just as many people in real life choose to exterminate snakes or wasps' nest rather than live in co-existence with them.

Thus, at another level, either—or logic is a perversion of our own awareness and psychological realities therein.[7] Its use, even unknowingly, confers some special status that simply doesn't exist. Thus, atheists are not out and out "goats" nor are Christians (or any other form of believer!) out and out "sheep". Rather both are human with intrinsic flaws and character defects that make them each a goat-sheep hybrid!

7. Affirming the Consequent

During more than one debate I've had with religionists over the years, I've been informed at some point:

> "God is real, It interacts with us regularly, and sometimes leaves corroborating evidence in Its wake. *Your problem is that you have refused to acknowledge it or even look for it!*"

In fact the assorted believers invoking this have committed the logical fallacy of affirming the consequent. They start out by stating that which they need to prove or demonstrate. In addition, they commit another logical error in assuming humans are "manifestations" of a deity. This is a trick often trotted out, particularly in the course of heated debates, and many times an unwary atheist will fall for it.

Here's the deal: the laws of deductive logic used in an argument, prevent a person from affirming that which he must *prove*. It doesn't matter if what's being affirmed happens to be visiting aliens from an advanced civilization on a planet of Tau Ceti, or some vague "intelligent designer" presumed to be responsible for the intricacies of the inner ear or the human eye, or an invisible, all-powerful and eternal Being.

---

7.   On another level, the reader should bear in mind that non-commutativity of operators in Hilbert space also gave rise to *"quantum logic"* wherein either-or considerations are no longer applicable. One can have both. This is addressed elsewhere in this text.

In each and every case the claim has to be presented as a conclusion to rigorous propositions or deductions, not stated as fact from the outset. Even the lesser claim that "evidence is left in its wake" amounts to an affirmation of the consequent. How did this evidence get there? What is its precise nature? How does one discriminate it, say from evidence bound to the natural order? (Since we are presuming evidence left by a God would be supernatural in character).

Nowhere is this more apparent than in the Intelligent Design (ID) arguments. ID's core problem was once articulated by astrophysicist Carl von Weizsacker who observed:

> "It is impossible to understand rationally a god whom one did not believe in already."

The problem is that spiritual second sight cannot be passed off as any kind of scientific process. The observed effect or material marvel, no matter how wondrous or incredible or beyond human conception, cannot be fobbed off as evidence for a "designer". Thus, if 'ID' is to be taken seriously it must compete on the same level playing field as bona fide scientific theories. That means first establishing a base of facts and evidence *unique to itself*. Then, formulating testable predictions which can be made—and that turn out to be more accurate than those of naturalistic evolution.

Until ID's proponents accomplish that, preferably in the context of publishing in established scientific journals, it will remain rank speculation along the lines of little green men surveying the Earth in flying saucers.

In the end, intelligent design inevitably amounts to an argument from ignorance. Because a structure (e.g. eardrum) or process (origin of life from inanimate matter) appears difficult from the inferior vantage point of the percipient, it's automatically assumed that no scientific appeal can be made. No model, however remotely probable, can be offered. Thus "intelligent design" is latched on to as a "god of the gaps". But history shows how absurd and premature such an approach is.

Ultimately, the problem for ID, when you strip away all the scientific jargon and window dressing, is that its base premise comes down to the logical fallacy of: *ignotum per ignotius* ('seeking to explain the not understood by the less well understood"). In this case, attempting to account for alleged "failures" of evolution or some claimed aspects not yet fully explained by to totally unknown constructs (e.g. 'supernatural' or unknown "designer"). This isn't science, it's hogwash and supernatural drivel disguised in the wardrobe of science.

But because organs such as the ear and eye *do appear* so astounding in complexity, many people fall like clay pigeons for affirming the consequent arguments that their mere existence points to an "intelligent designer", which, of course, must be supernatural in origin.

The other irritating aspect of ID proponents' affirming the consequent arguments is how they use perceived deficiencies in evolution as *positive affirmation* for ID. As if their recounting of these alleged deficiencies alone comprises an entire alter-proposal. It does not. They must abstract and disclose the agency for their alter-process, and this they have not done.

It would be analogous to me finding fault with umpteen aspects of Einstein's general relativity, and then somehow imagining that this recitation of *negativity* alone constitutes a genuine alternative theory. It doesn't, it only shows I have bones to pick with Einstein's theory. To have a genuine counter theory I must therefore provide a *positive* mathematical and observational infrastructure to counter Einstein's.

Thus:

Einstein asserts that $(X \pm x)$ accounts for the magnitude of advance of Mercury's perihelion per century[8], where X is the observed value and $\pm x$ the uncertainty.

I say, it is $(Y \pm y)$.

---

8.   "Perihelion" is the closest point of the planet to the Sun in its orbit. Einstein found that this point advances by about 43" per century, e.g. 43 seconds of arc where 1 second = 1/3600 degree. Thus, X = 43" here.

Einstein says that the solar oblateness[9] will be 1 part in W. I say it will be 1 part in Z. And so on and so forth. When ID can accomplish something analogous to this, in effect escaping its affirming the consequent loop, it may deserve be taken as more than gibberish and malarkey. Until then, one may rightly regard it as creationism decked out in new window dressing, with lots of scientific noises and sounds to baffle the befuddled.

8. Personal attack.

When all else fails, personal attack or ad hominem is most often invoked. Can't attack the arguments because they're airtight? No problem! Attack the man making them. Get the audience to believe he's the next thing to the Devil, if not the spawn of the Devil and maybe a cousin of Hitler or Stalin! Such disgusting tactics work because humans haven't fully left their reptilian brains behind. Those primitive regions (Carl Sagan once referred to it as the 'R-complex') remain in play and also, perniciously, capable of hijacking language to use as hateful rhetoric.

I recall one particular debate in 1989, when my opponent (A Scripture teacher) actually asked the audience:

> "How can we be certain he isn't possessed by Lucifer and doing Lucifer's bidding? As we know, seductive words are the hallmark of the Evil One. I am here to debate a human, but clearly it is useless if that human is really guided by a dark principality!"

Of course, this is the ultimate personal attack. If I'm tarred by association with Satan, however remotely, then I'm not to be given the most minute attention. My words can't be trusted because I am an "agent of Satan", to be dismissed and despised.

On another occasion, in the course of an intense 1990 debate with five or so Christians in *The Barbados Nation* newspaper, one of my attackers reprimanded

---

9.   "Solar oblateness" is the ratio of the polar (e.g. pole to pole) to the equatorial diameter. In a perfect sphere this ratio = 1.0. Solar oblateness always shows that the numerator is LESS than the denominator and hence the Earth betrays a degree of asymmetry with a "bulge" at its equator.

the editors for publishing so many of my letters and thereby "giving so much prominence to the views of an atheist".

In other words, my expressed views merited no benediction and certainly no coverage on the Op-Ed page, because I was an atheist. Not because I was bigoted or my arguments flawed.(Which they weren't). One wonders what this same Christian would have done if the roles were reversed, and five or six atheists belabored him. Would he be happily content to have a 5:1 letter ratio consistently published to give his opponents the podium edge? Or would he (reasonably) want as many letters to be published that he could write in response to any detractors?

Hypocrisy, of course, is never more blatant than when fueled by self-righteousness.

9. Sob story.

I confess that I've never been on the receiving end of this line of false argument, so can't really imagine the results. I have, however, seen other atheists given the short end of the sob story stick and it isn't pretty. The last time was at an American Atheists National Convention in 2001, in Orlando, Florida. During one session, an AA member voluntarily debated with a Christian minister. Bad idea.

The guy, as I recall, started right out of the block with nonsense not dissimilar to a Roman Catholic priest who once argued in the Barbados papers[10]:

"If Barbadians are misguided enough to stumble down the slippery slope of death before life and contempt for the innocent where Mr. X is leading us, we will be rejecting the most fundamental of the values which make this society Christian and it will not be long before we find ourselves defending people like William B. Waddell of Orange County, California, who in March 1977, strangled with his bare hands the infant of an 18-year old girl when saline solution failed to kill it."

---

10.   "No to Nightmare World," p. 8, *The Barbados Advocate*, July 2, 1990.

In other words, cry me a river! Keep atheists at the margins of society because, lo and behold, if their line of thinking gains prominence, all bets are off. We revert to mindless savagery, butchery, and incivility. How would a normal person's family or children ever be able to cope with such a monstrosity? What hope could one have for the future?

Tears and more tears.

Conveniently, the more emotion, anger and tears elicited the less room for reason or genuine debate. But this is the goal of the 'sob story' tactic: to arouse such heated emotions (and perhaps sobs) that they blind one to the content of the arguments.

To conclude, it should be obvious that the above fallacies need not be totally compartmentalized or isolated from each other. For example, a 'sob story' tactic can also have elements of personal attack, as well as red herring. Either/or reasoning can also embody affirming the consequent (or the converse). *Ignotum per ignotius* can be used in begging the question, or arguing from authority. The basic pattern of all these fallacies and their usages is more 'mix and match' than pick one and not the others.

The critical point for the beginning atheist engaged in argument, is to be able to quickly identify which tactic is being used against him, and the best way to respond. More often than not, the latter comes only by dint of hard work and much practice!

Summary point:

Most arguments with Christians, or theists in general, are based on their use of logical fallacies. The job of the diligent atheist is to be able to recognize what specific fallacy occurs in a given circumstance, and how best to respond. The best resource for doing this is perhaps Antony Flew's *Thinking About Thinking*, Fontana/Collins, UK, 1975. It provides a compendium of all the logical fallacies and how best to deal with each.

Short of that, atheists need to bear in mind that ninety percent of logical fallacy debates center on the meaning of "cause" or "causality" in a particular context. For example, "Is God a First Cause?" The problem is that most people don't even have a clue what is meant by cause, or how difficult it can be to parse or isolate single causes. Often, when one beholds some outcome or event, say a car crash, it is the result of a disjunctive plurality of causes: that is multiple causes acting in concert. Perhaps the driver had an elevated blood alcohol level after consuming five Margaritas, plus the treads were worn on the rear tires, plus another driver in the accident did not yield the right of way, plus there was a slow leak of brake fluid, plus the streets were icy, etc.

Because of the difficulty in identifying specific causes here, most of those who employ rigorous logic prefer the use of *conditions* to causes. Of particular interest, are what we call "necessary" and "sufficient" conditions. A necessary condition is one which, if absent, the presumed outcome is impossible. A sufficient condition is one which, if present, the presumed outcome must occur.

In the case of the car crash, a necessary condition would be that the car is being driven on the highway at all. If the car wasn't driven then no accident could happen. A sufficient condition for the crash (say after a thorough investigation) might be that the driver's blood alcohol level was over 0.5.

A more general and current example is human-induced global warming, which is now ramping up to planet-threatening proportions. A necessary condition for global warming is the presence of enough CO_2 already in the atmosphere. Another necessary condition is that a continuous source of replenishment must be available, since atmospheric CO_2 lasts one hundred years on average. It turns out that the CO_2 from fossil fuel combustion provides such a continuous source.

The sufficient condition for warming to occur on the scale documented is a self-sustained *positive feedback* loop. The basis has already been described by Sagan and others: Melting of ice caps (already occurring) results in diminished albedo (reflection of solar radiation back into space), and a darker Earth surface—with more infrared (or heat energy) absorbed, enhancing global warming. As more ice melts from the polar regions, positive feedback proceeds faster, ultimately becoming non-linear whereupon the effect becomes essentially unstoppable. In this case, one can only look forward to the *runaway Greenhouse effect*, which already converted Venus into the hellhole it is, since its proximity to the Sun alone can't account for temperatures hot enough to melt lead.

Given these illustrations, I am sure the reader can think of many others. The ability to do this will enable any unbeliever to more cogently argue with assorted theists, irrespective of their proposed deity.

The questions then that the atheist must pose to the theist are:

1. What exactly are the *necessary* conditions for your God to exist?

2. What exactly is the *sufficient* condition for your God to exist?

Interestingly, these questions in tandem also lay the foundation for a definition of "God." Of course, this is exactly what theists of all stripes (except perhaps the supporters of the holographic versions) have studiously avoided! Nevertheless, without at least a definition in place, to at least set limits of argument and debate, there is absolutely no hope of having a meaningful exchange.

This is a point that the intelligent atheist would do well to bear in mind: "Don't originate (or engage in) arguments that are open-ended, because your opponent has not defined his key term!"

4

Toward An Atheist Mindset

1. Back to God-Concepts:

At last count, there were close to 2,200 religions on the planet. More than ninety-nine point nine percent claimed to be the "only true" way to the light. All the others were pretenders, or frauds. Obviously, either truth is not an absolute commodity, or there are 2,200 lying religions. How can anyone know?

Worse, what does this say for the forlorn person born into a particular religion-say Catholic, and simply baptized as a *fait accompli* with no input or premeditated choice? What it tells me is that *all* religions are mere *potential temporary stops* on the path to a fuller insight, or enlightenment. Only a madman or fool would choose to "get off at the first stop" without examining or comparing any others.

Yet this rational stance is viewed as somehow heretical or a betrayal of one's family or parents' values. Now, I can and will grant (to some extent) the latter, but that is merely because one is inevitably born into one's parents' religion! Thus, in my own case, within six months of my birth in Milwaukee, my devout Catholic parents carted me off to the parish church, and had me baptized. Eight years later I had to make my first confession, and communion. Four years after that it was confirmation. And so on. My point is that at the time, all of this was followed as more or less expected ritualized behavior. No thought or choice went into it! No one asked me if I wanted that baptism, far less first communion!

After my marriage, I said "*Enough!*" and left the Church. My parents expressed shock, dismay, betrayal and resentment. "*How could you?*" they asked. *No one ever before in our family has ever left the Church and certainly never been an unbeliever!*

Feeling snarky at the time, since I'd been subjected to months of criticism on this, I retorted:

> "Perhaps because no one in the family ever scored in the top one percent of IQ tests before, and hence, possessed the mental wherewithal to examine and confront what he'd been born into!"

This shocked them even more, and hurled us into a prolonged period wherein all contact ceased: one of the unmentioned perils of "coming out of the closet" as an atheist. Nonetheless, beneath the cynicism of my response, they knew I was correct.

Too many, born into a condition, refuse to acknowledge it isn't their choice in the first place. How could it be, when they're manipulated through a series of rituals without being allowed to choose at any stage? The tragedy is that their life and personal identity ends up being hollow: *their parents religion* foisted onto them by a mere accident of birth!

But if one is going to be diligent about intellectual examination of his choices, where does s/he start? What sort of basis does s/he use? How can one arrive at a choice of religion from this, or a choice of being an atheist or not?

In Chapter One, I noted that the use of the term God-concept implicitly acknowledges a finite human intelligence to confront an ostensibly "infinite" entity. The basis for this is a mix of common sense and what I call a realist's insight. Obviously then, if a brain or even vast collection of brains amounts to a finite set, it will have severe problems grasping an "infinity," especially if this is deemed a deity with real existence

Invariably, God-concepts are flawed and limited because they're *abstracted* from a personal background of awareness and conditioning—as opposed to a total comprehension of actual being. In other words, the lack of understanding of the underlying entity (assuming there is one to understand) renders all concepts relative! There is simply insufficient information to distinguish one person's deity as the "one true God" to the exclusion of all others. This means that the Jewish concept of Yahweh, the Muslim concept of Allah, the Hindu concept of Brahmin and the Christian concept of the Trinity all stand in the same ontological relation. From an informational point of view, none can be selected as "true" to the exclusion of the others.

This is completely analogous to there being inadequate information to distinguish one religion's claims as true—to the exclusion of all others. In the case of individual religions, or religious traditions, the embodiment of the respective truth claim is found in a "sacred revelation", or holy book. For example, the Holy Bible for Christianity, the Talmud for Jews, the Koran for Muslims and the Upanishads for Hindus. The problem is that the early writers, for each scripture, suffered from the same limitation of comprehension that their modern counterparts do. Their neural capacity was just as finite as that of present-day humans, and just as conditioned toward a particular conceptual allegiance.

The upshot of the preceding relativism is that *all religions are on the same ontological footing!* It doesn't matter what any given one claims, or what special manuscripts, dogmas or rituals it invokes. No religion carries a larger embodiment of objective truth than any of its counterparts, because all originated within the same limited brain capacity of humans[1]! This means that, in the end, it makes no difference what religion one *chooses*—if one must choose a religion at all. Having said that, I would add (axiomatically) that if one *must* have a religion, it is far better to make a reflective and conscious choice than have it handed to you by birth as a fait accompli.

But what if one wishes to get beyond the human artifact of religion entirely? After all, the psychologist Carl Jung once said: *"Religion is a defense against the experience of God."* So even in the context of belief, organized religion is counterproductive.

The outcome (in any case) is that *the question of the existence* of any said infinite deity is certainly unanswerable. There are two sensible approaches that are left in the wake of this sober conclusion:

1. To treat supposed infinite deity as if it doesn't exist at all. (Often called the "approach of reversed effort")

2. To approximate it via an artifact tailored to a limited mind, or set of minds, and render it a God-concept.

---

1.   This has to do with *Godel's Incompleteness Theorems*, discussed elsewhere in this text.

The first of these is clearly the path of atheism or a type of atheistic agnosticism. Again, there is no "denial" at work here, merely the pragmatic admission that one is chasing a phantom by chasing an infinite deity with a finite mind. One could as well use one's time to search for leprechauns or the Loch Ness Monster.

The second might be said to be the path of the realist religionist or the theistic agnostic. Yes, a God may exist—even infinite and eternal—but our minds are too limited to grasp it in any fundamental way. Therefore, it's better to admit that when one uses the noun 'God', one is referencing the limited concept and not the actual Being. This is an admission of intellectual humility. An admission that human brains are too diminished in capacity and function to access the fundamental answers to life—or to have an exclusive grasp of the "one, true God", somehow denied to all those of other faiths.

In either case: concept ignored, or embraced and used—the objective is to distinguish the nearly universal allegiance to God-concepts from the separate issue of the factual existence of a deity. In other words, the widespread use and appeal of God-concepts does not necessarily mean that there is a genuine correspondent to reality, supernatural or otherwise.

In fact, humanity's penchant for articulating God-concepts could be dictated by brain architecture. The prevalence of God-concepts therefore reflects certain propensities or innate characteristics associated with the brain's hard wiring, rather than an "unconscious recognition of God". One of the most compelling lines of research in the past half century has been that of Julian Jaynes. In his 1976 work, *The Origin of Consciousness in the Breakdown of the Bicameral Mind*, Jaynes discussed the brain activity of ancient, pre-agrarian peoples.

He noted the ancient brain's lack of individual identity as well as a sense of metaphor. Probably a lot had to do with the necessity of living in collectives and always *acting* in the collective sense, whether hunting, sleeping, or moving to a new habitat. In this prehistoric setting, any frightening manifestations (say enormous lightning bolts that knocked down trees) would have been consciously invested with "divine" properties. Over many thousands of years, these associations would be engrained in the actual tissue of the brain. Jaynes speculated that more than a few of these "synaptic leftovers" could be embedded in our own brains. Possibly, they are the stuff from whence God-concepts arise, or at least the need to articulate them.

An exceptionally convincing line of research is that of Michael Persinger, of Laurentian University, Sudbury, Ontario, in Canada.[2]

Persinger found that when he electrically stimulated the temporal lobes of his subjects, a "religious experience" resulted. Some of the subjects claimed to be "in contact with God" while others experienced a profound sense of unity with the cosmos, and others a feeling of immortality. None of these was an external, objective experience. All originated from the brain's temporal lobes following localized electrical discharge. Persinger's experiments reveal, if nothing else, the human brain's complicity in inducing its own transcendent experiences. These experiments certainly do not refute the existence of a possible, real God, but they show that humans must proceed with extreme caution whenever claims concerning a deity are made.

Reinforcing this are the most recent results from neuropsychology and how the brain works. It is worthwhile pointing out that 95% of what neuroscience knows about the brain has been found out in the past 17 or so years. One of these facts is that there is a time delay between sensory perception (e.g. of the external world) and the conscious recognition of it. It is as if the brain is waiting a brief time "to decide whether to make the event aware to consciousness or not", in the words of Robert Ornstein.[3] In that half-second delay, Ornstein notes, there is also opportunity for the brain to "fabricate reality". In conjunction with Persinger's research, a question naturally arises: How much of religious experience—or what is called religious experience—is fabricated in a specific way by brains—say, in response to catechetical or other inputs from their religions? How much of contemporary religious experience and even the yen to find God depends upon the brain's "synaptic leftovers"—from the breakdown era of the ancient bicameral mind?

If the nearly universal need to believe in or worship a deity is grounded in brain architecture or operation then I think scientists, and indeed the general

---

2. Michael Persinger. 1983: *The Neuropsychological Bases of God Belief.*
3. Robert Ornstein.:1991, *The Evolution of Consciousness*, Random House, New York, p. 149.

population, must know about it. It is too important not to investigate scientifically, especially since the findings could be valuable in informing a conscious perspective on the issue. Such investigations might also shed light on why a minority group (atheists, agnostics) do not share this need to worship or formulate God-concepts. Do they lack the requisite brain chemicals or wiring? Or, is there a brain self-stimulation dynamic present in believers' temporal lobes that is absent in temporal lobes of unbelievers? Could this be traced to a gene, or complex of genes?

Twin studies already disclose "50 percent of religiosity (demonstrated by religious conviction and church attendance) can be attributed to genes."[4] Understandably, mention of such possibilities brings more than a little discomfort to those who are conventionally religious. Perhaps justifiably, they are aware that the discovery of a physical/chemical basis for religious belief could undermine the supernatural basis of most religions—if not many of their doctrines. As one Anglican priest in Barbados indicated to me after a debate I participated in: "It is preferable to leave the matter as a mystery of human existence, rather than to pursue it with scientific and impersonal ruthlessness."

I certainly understand this sentiment, though I do not agree with it. First of all, the issue concerns the paramount question of human existence, indeed *all existence*: Is there a supreme Being behind it all? For thousands of years the question has never been seriously considered because it was a "given," a no-brainer. Of course there has to be a God! How else could the universe exist! Now, however, the knowledge is genuinely available to probe more deeply into the ancient patterns of ritual, worship and belief that weave their way through all religious traditions.

The knowledge is available to re-frame the context of the question to make it more meaningful: Does the nearly universal worship of a deity proclaim the hidden truth that a deity actually exists?

This is an *answerable* question, as opposed to the unanswerable one of whether God actually exists. In terms of the above question, it would be a stupendous scientific discovery to learn that belief systems, including those of contemporary religions, evolved from the inner workings of the human brain.

---

4.   J. Neimark.: "Nature's Clones," in *Psychology Today*, August, 1997, p. 36.

For the first time, there is the opportunity to separate a pattern of human behavior from the underlying (assumed) divine entity that ostensibly motivates this behavior. Henceforth, in other words, the existence of deity cannot be guaranteed merely from observed patterns of human supplication or spiritual aspiration. It turns out to be a much more difficult thing to establish. This, I submit, is a positive benefit from the viewpoint of tolerance of others' beliefs and rituals.

At another level, there is the retrospective recognition that for thousands of years humans have functioned as the unwitting agents of their own brains' (or genes') excitations and tendencies. They've launched religious wars and crusades, as well as Inquisitions and legitimized intolerance, all as possible offshoots of neuro-chemical stimulations of their collective temporal lobes, or powerful genetic influences.

Given these defects, why wouldn't a person aspire to atheism, if for no other reason than to liberate one's psyche from the atavistic instincts of the brain? In this sense, a recognition that atheism = liberation is the first baby step to leaving all religious-God belief behind.

2. The Problem: Realism is in the Eye of the Beholder

Obviously, if the sensibility of God-concepts, the relativity of religions, and the dangers of being a slave to one's instincts were easily understood, everyone (just about!) would be an atheist. The fact that there are over 2,200 religions—most of which have ardent supporters—discloses that whatever mind virus carries religious belief is powerful indeed. So powerful that few people have the will and moxie to break free and liberate their minds. Because so few possess this freedom of mind, mostly atheists and some secularist freethinkers, it follows these people will bear the brunt of the believers' wrath. This is as it must be.

In his book, *The Lucifer Principle*, Howard Bloom[5] observes that while belief provides a sense of security to those who embrace particular memes, it also provides a ceaseless injunction to action to subdue opponents' beliefs. That is, to validate one's own beliefs all others must be attacked, criticized, impugned and

---

5.   Howard Bloom, *The Lucifer Principle: A Scientific Expedition into the Forces of History*, The Atlantic Monthly Press, 1995, p. 178.

preferably, eliminated. Throughout the ages various means have been developed to achieve this. In the case of Christianity it has been through the Inquisition and the Crusades. In the case of Islam, it's been achieved via harsh Sharia laws, or waging religious wars (jihads) against "infidels."

While it's easy to condemn both these manifestations of religious zealotry, it is important to know or understand why the respective zealots were so energized in the first place. It is highly doubtful, for example, that a Christian would kill a Muslim (or vice versa) based on their disagreement over the color of a distant star. So what drives the fervor?

The only plausible answer is that fundamental reality is at issue! Neither the Christian nor the Muslim is capable of accepting a wholly naturalist world such as atheists present. Such a world is anathema to them, because it lacks the necessities they regard as essential to their lives and beliefs. After all, they would have to face the dreadful combination of:

- Only one life to live, no afterlife. Hence "reward" or "punishment" in the eternal sense means nothing.

- No souls, only material bodies. Hence, there is nothing to save or survive death in the first place.

- No overriding cosmic force or "Creator" exists to demand a particular code of behavior.

- A meaninglessness of sin for all the above reasons.

This would be enough to enrage any zealot. Think of it! The Christian is denied the pleasure of sitting at the right hand of his God to see all the sinners and miscreants, not to mention unbelievers., tormented forever. Can't have that! The Muslim fanatic, meanwhile, is denied getting to be with those 72 virgins after committing some heinous act of jihad. Worse, there is NO ONE controlling the big cosmic machine! That means all those atheists and infidels can run loose, say what they want and *disbelieve* without worrying about afterlife consequences.

The issue then boils down to: What type of reality do humans accept? There are only two possible basic answers:

1. A wholly natural reality, operating according to natural laws that have either: a) already been discovered (e.g. entropy law, law of gravity) or will be discovered.

2. A supernatural reality, which allows novel and emergent entities and phenomena that don't fall under natural laws.

In the first case, no matter how many different phenomena we observe or measure, we will find that mass-energy is conserved; heat transfers from hotter to colder bodies, any time you combust gasoline in an auto engine you can't re-process the fumes into new gasoline; light (or information) cannot propagate faster than 300,000 kilometers per second, and whatever is tossed off a height falls under the influence of gravity. Also, no one can walk on water, water can't be changed into wine, and the dead can't be brought back to life. Nor can a pound of fish be suddenly converted into ten pounds or a thousand.

All these disclose the limits of physical or natural laws. If these limits were violated, even occasionally, we would have to face the fact of supernaturalism operating at some level. However, no documented cases of any of these have held up. When weird, freakish events are reported (e.g. of the "Fortean" category), all the evidence is anecdotal, meaning none is replicable. What this shows, is that the naturalist reality is the one we inhabit.

An oft-cited example of supernatural reality is the so-called miracle at Fatima. According to common themes in the mass of reports taken on October 13, 1917, the following events occurred:

- The "Blessed Virgin" (long since deceased) appeared around noon and said that people ought to recite the rosary daily

- The "Sun" (or some object resembling it) began to spin on its axis like a pinwheel

- Streamers of light erupted from its rim and splashed across the sky

- It then stopped spinning, then resumed—hurling out different colors each time

- The "Sun" then left its position and commenced to advance toward the Earth—or so it appeared. It grew larger and larger, the heat increasing all the while.

- As the immense "Sun" retreated, people breathed a sigh of relief and noted that their clothing was soaking wet.

All of the above bear the hallmarks of delusion, not reality. There is simply no way the Sun could undergo any of these manifestations without the entire world knowing of it. To believe so, is to believe that 3 billion people around the world were simultaneously placed into a temporary (~ 4 minute) mass coma—including lost time—while the 'select few' thousands at Fatima managed to actually behold reality and the Sun's antics. This is pure poppycock and baloney.

To compound this, no extant solar observatory records disclose any unusual behavior from the Sun that day. There were no gymnastic gyrations in the sky. There were no prominences erupting hundreds of millions of miles to be actually visible from Earth. Nor did the Sun suddenly get displaced closer from its normal position, changing the distance to the Earth (which would have permanently altered the Earth's orbit to a very precarious one!)

Recall David Hume's words from earlier:

"No testimony is sufficient to establish a miracle, unless the testimony be of such a kind that its falsehood would be more miraculous than the fact which it endeavours to establish."

Let's see how that might be applied to the alleged events at Fatima. The question is: Would the falsehood (of those events) *be more miraculous* than any facts it attempted to establish?

Such falsehood would imply that more than 70,000 reported observers either were all lying through their teeth, or were all simultaneously under the same spell. This is certainly pretty far out, and in fact darn near incredible! But, does that vanishing small probability mean that the events *took place as claimed?* Not at all.

While it is definitely improbable so many thousands could be wrong in their reports, *it is more improbable* that all the solar observatories in the world were tricked, and all their telescopes instantly ceased working. It is also more improbable that the Sun could actually move toward Earth then back, without permanently altering Earth's orbit and wreaking havoc worldwide that no one seemed to report! Thus, the improbability of tens of thousands being wrong is trumped by the improbability that the Sun actually misbehaved and no solar astronomers were any the wiser, not to mention nearly 3 billion humans!

What could have happened then? French astronomer Jacques Vallee provides one of the most audacious explanations based on how many items the Fatima events have in common with typical UFO sightings.[6] He concludes that the "Sun" was not the real Sun at all, but a brilliant disc or UFO which displayed aspects including "falling leaf trajectory and heat wave" that are "frequent parameters of UFO sighting everywhere".

In a related context, Vallee addresses the "miracle" at Lourdes. The events at Fatima and Lourdes contain inherent elements of absurdity at which the rational mind rebels. In the Fatima case, the Sun is supposedly bounced around like a ball even while observatories worldwide reported no unusual solar phenomena. Vallee notes that at Lourdes, Bernadette is told by an apparition to wash herself in a non-existent spring and to "eat the grass that grows there". Current accounts of alien abductions are equally preposterous, with the aliens passing through walls, performing clumsy sexual examinations and blood tests, and attempting to harvest ova from American suburbanite matrons for cross-breeding. Could both types of event emanate as signals from the same source?

This seems likely, though no one will claim it's prosaic. The point to emphasize here is that while a UFO explanation is certainly fairly far out, the alternative explanation of the Sun performing numerous hijinks with no one recording or observing them is even moreso! So, pick your poison! For me, I will take the UFO as the less mentally corrosive poison!

What about the appearance of the Blessed Virgin? Given that UFO-nauts probably have the capacity to do anything (since they've obviously traveled light years to get here) who says they can't generate holograms too? In this case, it is fairly possible they might have generated a hologram of Our Lady by tapping into stored memories in the Fatima crowd's collective brains, and maybe elaborating them a bit to a homogenized, stable vision.

---

6.   Jacques Vallee: "The Physics of the BVM," in *Dimensions*, Ballantine Books, 1988.

So no one misinterprets this, I'm not saying I accept the UFO thesis either. Or that aliens actually came into close contact with Earthlings at Fatima on October 13, 1917! I am only saying that of the two explanations proffered—supernatural vs. non-prosaic but natural—the latter is the one to be preferred. If at such time an even better one (and hopefully more prosaic) arrives, I'll be the first to embrace it!

3. The Nitty-Gritty: Realism vs. Idealism

Having provided concrete examples of the differences between naturalism and supernaturalism, it's important to explore the underlying philosophies to understand why atheists dismiss miracles, afterlives, gods and other religious phantasmagorias. The two philosophies at issue here are known as *realism* and *idealism*.

As noted by Euan Squires[7], idealism is predicated on "the simple observation that all knowledge comes from sensations in the conscious mind. Thus, since everything I know, I know through my mind, it follows that in some way my mind is the only certain reality." The philosopher Antony Flew provides a broader underpinning by noting that idealism is not a single philosophy, but rather a group of philosophies, all of which have in common the notion that what humans call "the external world" is somehow created by the mind.[8]. The most extreme representative of this school is probably personified by Immanuel Kant, in his book "*A Critique of Pure Reason.*"

In more modern times, idealism persists, often in the guise of Derridian "deconstruction," which insists all truth is relative to the percipient. This supposedly engenders some irreducible solipsism that renders all scientific work more subjective than objective. Carried to its ultimate conclusion, all confidence in the scientific method is impaired, since all data and observation are contaminated by subjectivity and self-reference. One can never apprehend the "pure external phenomenon" so why even delude oneself into thinking it is possible or achievable? Of course, one pronounced effect of this is an epistemological castration of science. With the scientific method castrated, it can't be used to investigate whether

---

7.   Euan Squires: *Conscious Mind and the Physical World*, Adam Hilger Books, p. 74.

8.   Antony Flew: *A Dictionary of Philosophy*, St. Martin's Press, 1984.

or not alternative "realities" exist, or whether or not the cosmos is "emergent", or "transcendent" or has "meaning" or has a god looking after it.

A new twist on this theme is proposed by Pascal Boyer[9]. He shows that religious concepts invariably embody information that is "*counterintuitive to the category activated*". For example, Catholics insist that the consecrated bread is the real body of Christ (via a process called transubstantiation) although performing a protein and starch test quickly discloses said wafer to be 100% starch and not protein (flesh). The ontological category of "body" is definitely a flesh-bearing, biological entity that has cells etc. but the information in the concept ("the bread is a body") contradicts this!

The thrust of Boyer's position appears to be that skeptics may have serious trouble refuting religious concepts because of this barb of contradictory information within them. Perhaps, but stripped of the obscurantism what we really have is an idealistic argument that, because contradictions may appear in certain religious concepts, they'll more likely survive skeptical scrutiny. However, in the context of Gödel's Incompleteness theorems this simply doesn't hold. More on that later.

Perhaps the most damning indictment of idealism has been offered by Squires[10] who notes that: "the most useful argument against all such philosophies is that they discourage any endeavor to understand the sensations of the conscious mind." This is certainly true in so far as understanding is contingent on a reductionist approach, which idealism rejects in favor of holism as the Greek Stoics once did.

From the above overview, one can safely say that idealist philosophies, which invest a paramountcy or primacy in the "mind", have only disdain for scientific techniques applied to uncovering "dynamics of consciousness". Clearly then, any workable or testable theory of consciousness cannot come from idealism—but rather its alter ego: realism.

---

9. Pascal Boyer: 2001: *Religion Explained: The Evolutionary Origins of Religious Thought*, Basic Books, pp. 64-65
10. Squires, E.: *op. cit.*, p. 74.

In contrast to idealism, realism is the underlying philosophy of science. It asserts that human consciousness receives experiences from an external world, quite distinct from that consciousness. As Squires notes:[11] "The images we obtain, involving for example eyes, ears, telescopes, etc. are images of a genuinely existing reality whose existence is not dependent on our being aware of the images." Squires observes that in quantum mechanics, for example, there is an observer disturbance of the system, but "just because we observe and disturb it is not to say we create it."

According to Antony Flew[12], realism is the belief that physical objects exist independently of being perceived. (Or to paraphrase physicist N. David Mermin: "The Moon is really there when nobody looks!") Arguably, therefore the notion of an "observation" only has significance in the context of a realistic philosophy, just as the question "What exists?" In order to even think of asking the latter, the implicit inference must be that there is a real, externally persistent world.

More recent formulations of realism, in the wake of apparent nonseparability in quantum theory, differentiate between "naive realism" and "far realism". In naive realism, the "pure phenomenon" can be apprehended through instrumentation or measuring device with a minimum of observer disruption. In "far realism" observer disruption always accompanies observation and measurement, and in quantum mechanics this disturbance is arbitrarily large.

What has all this to do with supernaturalism, naturalism and examples discussed in Section 2? Simply this, that those who embrace an other-worldly philosophy are more likely to be idealists at heart. That is, endorse some aspect of idealist philosophy. They are far more likely to distrust the reductionist ways of hard science, and to find a place for faith.

Believing the events at Fatima is no problem, since the underlying (idealist) philosophy would simply assert that no unusual solar events were observed because none of the astronomers in the world *expected them to be*! Thus, either they didn't observe, period or—if they did—they dismissed what they saw, going into some kind of subconscious denial.

---

11.   Squires, E.: *ibid.*
12.   Flew, A.: *op. cit.*

Go back to N. David Mermin's famous realist statement: *"The Moon is really there when nobody looks!"* But, was the Sun? Specifically, on October 13, 1917?

In the idealism purview, neither Sun nor Moon may "be there" if no one looks to make sure. Thus, if no astronomers were observing that day in 1917, who's to say the Sun didn't go on vacation and have some frolic time? Bouncing around this way and that, and scaring the bejeebers out of seventy thousand frightened folk at Fatima.

Before any susceptible readers bite on this, I'd only ask you to think of your own homes. When you're away at work or shopping, is your home still there? Where you left it? Can you be certain? I mean you're not observing it, after all. If you can't be sure, then why on Earth waste gas driving back to it? It would seem to be an exercise in futility, or at least uncertainty! But this sort of lunacy is where pure idealism leads us!

Is it any wonder the naturalist and realist who objects often chooses the path of atheistic naturalism, even if he may not call it that? At the same time, there is a corollary to the idealist credo that something may not "be there" if no is looking at it. That is, even when you are looking at something, you may not see it! Spirits or ghosts anyone? Or how about devils, angels, hobgoblins, Bigfoot, leprechauns, fairies and.... you name it?

In line with this, the naturalist or scientific realist can only be a "fair witness" in hetero-phenomenological style: that is, whatever a believer or witness of anything strange: (UFO's, weeping madonnas, angels) tells him, the scientist's proper response is: "I believe that *you believe you saw.... heard.... experienced.... etc.*

Let's now return to Pascal Boyer's contention that religious concepts might pose problems for the ardent skeptic because of the inherent contradictions imbued in the language. I earlier made reference to Gödel's Incompleteness theorems.

Gödel's (incompleteness) theorems state that in any consistent system rich enough to produce simple arithmetic there are formulae (axioms or statements) that can't remain proven-in-the-system. Consider the simple statement of logical transitivity:

$$X = Y$$

$$Y = Z$$

$$\therefore X = Z$$

What if instead we append an axiomatic statement that reads, in effect: "X = Y is *unprovable*-in-the-system". If this statement is provable-in-the-system, we get a contradiction, since if it is provable in-the-system, then it can't be unprovable-in-the-system. This means the original axiom: "*X = Y is unprovable-in-the-system*" is false. Similarly, if X = Y is provable-in-the-system, then it's true, since in any consistent system nothing false can be proven in-the-system, only truths.

So the statement:-axiom: "X = Y is unprovable-in-the-system" is not provable-in-the-system, but unprovable-in-the-system. Further, if the statement-axiom "X = Y is unprovable in-the-system" is unprovable-in-the-system, then it's true that that formula is unprovable-in-the-system. Thus the statement, "X = Y is unprovable-in-the-system" is true.

With these preliminaries, let's examine the logical structure ascribed to most religious concepts. According to Pascal Boyer, we get a syllogism like:

If X, then Y

If X, then Z

so, Y = Z

But, $Z /\ Y$ (contradiction)

Example:
If a consecration (X) is performed, then a bread wafer (Y) becomes body or flesh (Z).
Bread wafer = body-flesh

But, actual chemical tests show the bread wafer is starch, not flesh or protein!

Religious concept:

The identity Y = Z refers to a statement of *substance*.

The contradiction Z/\ Y refers to the outcome of "accidents"
Thus, the statements embodying substance (S + 1) > S, where S denotes the axiomatic statements embodying the accidents.

We call such statements "meta-statements".

In a manner of speaking, the religious concept claimant is in a similar position to Epimenides in his "all Cretans are liars" paradox, which itself perpetuates a causal loop with no closure. E.g.

"All Cretans are Liars"

If the speaker is a Cretan, then the statement is ipso facto unresolvable. If Cretan, he exists within the so-called abstract, formal system. Yet, he's making a statement (meta-) *about the system.* Hence, is he lying? Or is he telling the truth? This cannot be resolved. An undecidable proposition, as Godel's Incompleteness Theorem (II) applies.

Is there a way out of the loop? Yes, if one uses realist science to assess statements. For example, in the Einstein equation, $E = mc^2$, scientific epistemology allows us to regard E, m and c as *constructs*, connected via *operational definition* to the P- (perceptual) facts of: energy, mass and the speed of light. Thus, we expect a correlation like:

$$C <\text{-}> P$$

This re-affirms logical closure, physical significance and no meta-linkage.

For instance, the operational definition of "mass" is accomplished by comparing inertias, using detected accelerations via m2/m1 = a1/a2 and Newton's 2nd law say in a collision or motion (down an inclined plane) experiment.

In effect, even if a science or research hypothesis may include some open or meta-statements (evidently leaving the room open for undecidable propositions) there are nevertheless empirical checks and tests that can close the system parameters. Nothing similar exists for supernatural claims embodied in religious concepts.

Consider the statement:

"This consecrated bread wafer is the body of Christ"

Here we have neither P-facts nor C-construct. There is no confirmatory device for example, to demonstrate that the bread before me is a *human body*. The statement is open-ended, and could also be delirium tremens or maybe the product of a micro-seizure in the brain's temporal lobes as researcher Michael. Persinger has shown.

Worse, we can't even identify unique and distinguishing attributes that point to the validation of the claim. Without even venturing into the realm of P-facts, the set of C-constructs ("bread",. "body of Christ") is ripe for self-reference as well as the intrusion of incompleteness with no available cross checks!

What if, instead, one ignores this, and assigns attributes willy-nilly? Say by insisting: "well you cannot detect the body because you are only able to ascertain base physical "accidents" (e.g. starch or carbohydrate composition) using scientific analyses. In this case the claimant commits reification. He imposes his preconceived *percepts* on what is in reality an open-ended field. For such an open field, discussion is fruitless, since it ends up being a mental Rohrshach for the benefit of the proponent.

By contrast, the advocate of $E = mc^2$ (e.g. from nuclear fission or fusion reactions) has no latitude or degrees of freedom to "fill in" anything, since all P-facts are already defined by specific constructs and operational definitions which have very exact meaning in physics. (e.g. c, the velocity of light, or about 300,000 km/sec) There is no wiggle room, and this lack of wiggle room means there exists predefined context, as well as escape from lurking Godelian loops.

In the end, we are entitled to reject the religious concept posed in contradictory or meta-language terms Though something is claimed (if only a possibility statement) the logical framework remains open since:

1. The claimant has not defined exactly what his terms mean

2. He lacks the critical, discriminatory P-facts to back up his claim; facts which can be confirmed outside his reference frame

3. He uses circular arguments to return to his original claim

On account of this, as Herman Philipse has noted, we may legitimately show respect for religions because they reflect deep human longings. However, we are not obliged to show any respect when they "put forward claims of knowledge".[13]

And so it was, fourteen years ago, when an excited person called me up (I was a science columnist for the Barbados *Advocate* at the time) to eagerly tell me that he'd seen an angel the night before. My reply: "Yes, I believe that you believe you saw an angel". Had he left it at that, all would have been well. Regrettably, the problem is that the memes of most believers do not allow them to "settle" for het-ero-phenomenological acceptance. He wanted *phenomenological* acceptance as well:

"No, no! You don't understand, I really *saw* an angel! It was right here in my room, right next to me—it smiled and spoke to me!"

At this point, the believer's transgression into claimed epistemology invited empirical accountability:

"Oh really? Do you have this on a camcorder? Or a photograph? Or, do you have the angel's voice on tape recorder at least? What have you got?"

"Well…. uh, nothing."

"Fine, but that's also what you get from me in return: nothing!"

At this point, we see the full manifestation of the atheist mindset: it accepts nothing on faith! There must be a measure of empirical (or other indirect empiri-cal, mathematical) accountability. This is because the mindset is grounded in the realist philosophy: that things actually do exist outside the human mind, and—more often than not—some means can be found to empirically validate them.

The theist's mindset works in the opposite direction: We can't know every-thing or provide evidence for most things, so must take the bulk on faith. Even science has its limits. Therefore, to err on the side of caution, accept the claim then try to prove it later.

---

13. H. Philipse.: Reason and Religion, in *Free Inquiry* (Feb./Mar. 2007), p. 37

The magic bullet that the theist (or believer of anything transcendent) uses is faith. For example, the faith meme (of which the god-meme is a derivative) has been likened by Richard Dawkins to a self-sustaining and self-protecting program[14]. It possesses self-reference to such a degree that it has built-in safeguards against detection or elimination. One of these memes is often heard expressed by the religious:

"Faith is superior to logic, because faith goes beyond logic in its approach to truth".

Hence, the person who "buys into" this meme, will value faith over his or her own logic, and not be willing to question that faith in logical terms. (Since faith is "superior"). One can say that the so-called "virtue" of faith is paradoxical since it requires "going beyond logic") With this high survival value, the faith meme, like the god-meme, can more easily "infect" other brains by replication. Or try to!

One of the best direct illustrations of this I ever saw occurred while watching a 1990 "Larry King" show on CNN. It featured rational skeptic Paul Kurtz (then Editor of *Free Inquiry* magazine) and the topic was "The Devil." Kurtz, along the same lines I used above, disputed that any such entity has ever existed, now or in the past. This was in contradiction to a priest on the same show, who claimed that he'd performed actual exorcisms of "demons". (Some clips of the alleged exorcisms were included, but Kurtz never bit. He pointed out that it appeared the "possessed" person was being held down, and anyone held down would fight like hell to get up!)

One of the first viewer phone calls came from a woman who took Kurtz to task for not believing in "Satan." So excited she could hardly contain the emotion in her voice, she blurted out: "You see? That's just what Satan wants. He wants people *not* to believe in him, so he can become more powerful."

This is a perfect example of a self-sustaining mind virus in action. Kurtz, the innocent rationalist and realist, was "empowering Satan" (in this poor woman's deluded mind) because he *declined to believe in him* or it.

---

14.   Richard Dawkins: *The Selfish Gene*, Oxford University Press, 1976, p. 35.

Numerous permutations on this theme have been documented, but all can be traced to the same power issuing from the same meme. Another variant is that "Satan is using skepticism" (or using logic) to try to get people to reject God. Which is really just a corollary on the axiom that "faith is superior to reason."(If faith is superior to reason, then skepticism must be inferior to faith, and one's mind can fall prey to disembodied entities or "powers and principalities.")

This ought to insult any halfway intelligent person. It presupposes that we're all mental invalids, incapable of using reason or logic to our own ends. Rather, some fantastic hidden entity ("Satan") is using this reason or logic for us—and perverting our conclusions. If we just didn't appeal to reason or logic we'd be all right, and would "see the light".

Seen in this light, the current cultural clash between faith and secularism on the nature of reality is really a clash between two large systems of memes: one representing science and empirical accountability, the other representing the dilution of that system by advocating the recognition of "self-reference", obscurantism, deconstruction, and the superiority of faith etc.

For anyone living amidst this clash, a clear position has to be embraced sooner or later. Sitting on the fence isn't an option, because the nature of reality isn't a matter of "choice". Either you accept that there is an objective world and real events happen within it, or you accept that it's all in someone's mind and perceptions are ultimately subjective.

The individual with the atheist mindset will always use reason, and base his or her life in objective reality and act knowing that a genuine, external universe exists independently of one's consciousness. Faith or belief has no place in such a mindset, because humans alone are accountable for their actions and responsible for their fate. No one can lay blame on a god or gods, and certainly not placing faith in such. The question remains: How many are really prepared to travel the road of an atheist? Or if one already is, come out of the closet to family and friends?

Summary points:

- An atheist mindset requires the consistent cultivation and use of reason.

- Michael Persinger's research exposes most religious phenomena as products of micro-seizures in the brain's temporal lobes. This is a useful premise for the atheist.

- At root, detailed religious abstraction seems to be a product of the philosophy of *Idealism*. Atheists, in contrast, prefer to operate using the philosophy of *realism*.

5

Atheists Aren't the Media's Darlings!

If one is determined to acknowledge oneself as an atheist, one must also be aware of the Zeitgeist that currently permeates American culture and society. In no small measure, the American Zeitgeist is determined by public relations (as opposed to fact), media depictions and outright bias.

In general, the corporate-owned media regard atheism as a disreputable and largely un-American philosophical position, only about one step removed from being a communist. If one disputes this, one need only dredge up the last twenty or so articles that have been published in the mainstream media about atheists or atheism. In general, these depictions are strongly biased and reinforce the negative imagery most Americans already have (as disclosed by one recent poll that most Americans would even choose a Muslim for president over an avowed atheist).

One relatively recent example was a small column by *Newsweek* columnist Lisa Miller (under the "Belief Watch" segment of Periscope, Oct. 30, 2006, page 12). While shining her media spotlight on atheist author Sam Harris, Miller wrote:

"… one is struck by how personable, how familiar he seems, a soft-spoken man with pleasant manners, a man who wrote two best selling books while pursuing a degree in neuro-science. He is, in other words, an unlikely infidel"

Of course, this passage dignifies and circulates the most vile stereotypes that the general population continues to believe about atheists. That we are unsocial, hostile, brash, and probably loud mouthed boors to boot, with few manners, and little in the way of education. Fortunately, the magazine had the intestinal fortitude to publish at least a couple letters in a subsequent issue that raked Miller's dubious approach over the coals. But Miller is by no means the only offender.

A few weeks later, a major article "The New Believers" appeared[1] which purported to highlight the recently published books of a number of high profile unbelievers, including: Sam Harris, Richard Dawkins, and Daniel C. Dennett. The article by Jay Tolson actually framed all the unbelievers as being extremists and unreasonable for their positions. Meanwhile, the religious apologists were uniformly depicted as eminent spokespersons of reason, who actually supported working to make America "a more civil society" while the unbelievers were out to do the opposite. The last line of the piece essentially framed these top atheists as a pack of boors only too willing to launch into fights at dinner tables!

None of this ought to surprise the atheist, either the one in the making or the established unbeliever. The cold, unimpeachable fact is that the media in the United States is outright hostile to atheists, and finds little about them that is commendable or worthwhile, even to warrant a positive article. The one small concession was a piece in *Newsweek*, "The Case Against Faith", by Sam Harris, in which he cogently argued how religion does untold damage to our national politics. Regrettably, most of the letters published in response to the piece were highly negative, basically accusing Harris of the same sort of "extremism" that Tolson painted with wide brush in his U.S. News article.

Even skeptical journals aren't immune from this sort of thinking, as in a recent piece ("Above Contempt*")* in *Free Inquiry* wherein Wendy Kaminer took atheists to task for assorted manifestations of extremes against the religious. Specifically, Kaminer wrote that she'd "hate to see notions of sin give way to dysfunction" while adding that we ("non-theists") should also not jettison evil or abstain from judgmentalism.

In a response letter, published in a subsequent issue, I noted all of Kaminer's terms are "hallmarks of the primitive, pre-scientific mind,"[2] despite Kaminer proclaiming herself a secularist. I went on to point out:

---

1.   *U.S. News and World Report*, Nov. 13, 2006, page 40.
2.   P.A. Stahl, "Religious vs. Secular Concepts", in *Free Inquiry*, April/May 2007, p. 65.

"For example, 'sin' is a fundamentally religious concept, which has no scientific or objective basis. Indeed, it is part of the religious mind virus or meme structure. Without the presumption of "sin," humans cannot be threatened with "damnation" and driven to seek redemption and refuge in religions."

I added that a true secularist would rely instead on *The Diagnostic and Statistics Manual*, which has a statistical-empirical scientific basis. Eschewing that, if one opted for "sin" over a diagnosed dysfunction then one clearly sympathizes with circulating religious memes.

In the same letter I also took Kaminer to task for her use of the loaded term *"evil"* which is also a primitive religious concept. The use of the word presumed origination from "a negative supernatural force" or "Satan". However, by the Ockham's Razor Principle (already cited earlier) one need not invoke this at all. It overly complicates the issue while unnecessarily adding theoretical existences. We already know in this case that ancient brain structures (e.g. amygdala, reticular formation etc.) can account for all atavistic behaviors from misdirected lust, to baby killing to mass murder or genocide. One need not invent a supernatural special being or super Devil to account for them!

Kaminer replied in a short note to my letter[3], basically averring she had no intention of altering her "attachment to moral categories of good and evil." This is her prerogative and right, of course, but doesn't alter my own point one iota. That is, that if Kaminer embraced such attachment then she is more rightly a *religionist* and not a secularist or humanist. Secular people refrain from using religious words, labels, concepts or language.

All this elicits the question: What is the committed atheist to do in order to survive and even prosper in a god-squad culture where even Super Bowl winning coaches point their fingers skyward and attribute their success to the "Lord"? Here are some suggestions:

1. Be an active participant not a doormat:

Despite the fact that most media in the U.S. are hostile to unbelief, the majority will still publish occasional letters to the Editor from atheists, provided you

---

3.   Wendy Kaminer, ibid.

are persistent. Over the years, I have had at least a half dozen articles published in *The Baltimore Sun*, as well as a full column in *The Baltimore Evening Sun*. These showed in no uncertain terms that there are real, live atheists in this country and they aren't afraid to speak or write their mind. I have also, incredibly enough, had atheist letters published in *The Colorado Springs Gazette*, though not as often as I'd like. Never mind, the fact I've been able to get even three or four published in a bastion of conservative religious fundamentalism shows there is hope.

This is not to say that the publication of atheist viewpoints will go unchallenged. Indeed, after my *Baltimore Evening Sun* piece appeared, scornful, mostly illegibly written letters poured in from across the Bible Belt. Each irate writer, from a granny in North Carolina, to a farmer in Georgia, felt they were bound by "God's hand" to set this outlandish 'feller' straight. One tome surpassed 13 pages, laden with mostly incomprehensible script that amounted to one long harangue after another. Most ended up in the nearby dumpster.

Similarly, after each letter published in the local Gazette, at least 3-4 counter letters were published, reflecting the views of extreme fundamentalists and evangelicals. I don't mind that there are responses, but it would be great if a "let's gang up on him" dynamic didn't rear its ugly head each time!

My point is not to let detractions intimidate you. It's far more important to get the word out that the atheist viewpoint is real and exists and that real people are prepared to advance it.

Another approach, when you find your local paper is not publishing, is to try for a national arena. The *Newsweek* volunteer column 'My Turn' is a good example, though I will say that I have never been published there, despite a number of attempts. But who knows? If the right atheist approaches the task with the right mindset, it could be an opportunity to command lots of eyes.

Failing that, the last resort is to directly e-mail the authors of pieces you find offensive. In most major newspapers their e-mails are given at the end of the column. I have found this is an excellent 'stick' when called for. However, I make sure I don't overdo it. Usually one good, cogent sound-off is enough and make sure you don't go into a long rant or harangue. Keep it short and to the point, and try to avoid ad hominems!

2. Think of starting local chapters or workshops:

Another excellent idea, which was presented to me at the 2001 Atheist Convention in Orlando, is to start local atheist chapters or even workshops. In the first instance, you may be able to align with 'Freethinker' groups in your area and even use their facilities. See about getting guest speakers, say famous national or state atheists, to present a talk or give a seminar (if considering a workshop).

A two or three night series could do wonders in raising consciousness at many levels locally and make the work "atheist" a despised impersonal (and despised!) term than it now is. It's also possible, if press releases are sent out, to get the local newspaper to cover it and thereby provide more insights for the community at large. Just be sure to ask to check the copy before it goes to press, to ensure the reporters get their facts straight and aren't out there attempting to frame atheism in a biased way. "Freelancing" is okay, up to a point.

Don't forget or neglect the value of interviews either, especially if you're one of the few atheists in the community prepared to make him/herself known! Always also ask to see a transcript of the interview as soon as possible, and check to make sure it's accurate. Misrepresentation of atheists is so common in the society now that many reporters aren't even conscious of what they're doing.

None of these approaches is easy, but they're essential if we're to penetrate the pervasive prejudice that currently exists against Atheists. Every step in this campaign helps, none is too small or too trite to attempt. The other good thing is by going out and taking such action, others of like mind will make themselves known.

Summary points:

- The mainstream (corporate) media are largely hostile to atheism and also atheists, treating them like so many errant children at best, and as anti-American threats at worst. The atheist must expect this sort of dismissive attitude, and understand the media are largely conforming to the hostile mass mind syndrome endemic in the culture.

- The corporate media's abhorrence of atheism has even filtered into many secularist venues, causing them to either sugar coat positions or invite many more "moderate" secularists to write articles for them.

- Despite the difficulties, atheists can still fight back to an extent, by writing letters in response to perceived misrepresentations, or to simply sound off.
- Atheists always have the ability to organize local groups and conduct educational meetings, with the view to expanding public outreach and hence, understanding. All of these efforts can be used as a basis to invite the local media in for coverage, and hence garner positive attention for atheists.

6

Do You Really *Want to be An Atheist?*

1. To Use or Not to Use the "A-word"

Let's cut right to the chase: the term "atheist" is now the most reviled epithet in the English language, yet it's used to describe (technically) someone who simply withholds belief in a deity. One would think, to behold some of the revulsion (especially in the right wing press and on right wing talk shows) that "atheist" denoted some new kind of perverse sex criminal or predator.

Why this intense hatred simply for disbelief? It's important to address this before one can deal with the question of whether (or not) to call oneself an atheist.

Biochemist Jacques Monod probably comes as close as anyone to a decent answer in his chapter, 'The Kingdom and the Darkness' in his book *Chance and Necessity*. He notes that the "prodigious developments of knowledge" over the past three centuries or so have forced an "agonizing reappraisal of Man's concept of himself".

This knowledge is based on objectivity and reductionism, which on the one hand conferred enormous material power and efficacy. But on the other hand sowed the seeds for destruction of all the hitherto accepted myths, and especially supernatural beliefs. None of which could withstand the scrutiny of science's "postulate of objectivity". For, at root, when one looks simply at the basic infrastructure and methods of science, it is a wholly value-less enterprise. In this enterprise, as we saw, all supernatural additions and confabulations turn out to be so much superfluous dross. To use Monod's words[1]:

In the course of three centuries, science, founded upon the postulate of objectivity, has won its place in society in men's practice. But not in their hearts.

Sure, there've been weak attempts to patch over this chasm, but all of them are transparent. The most recent one is the religious' acceptance of evolution as "God's means to create the universe". Of course, this is nonsense. At root, the naturalist theory of evolution in its full mold of natural selection and mutation has no need of any external agents, especially supernatural ones!

External agents do not enhance our predictions or explanations (from genetics), nor do they help refine methods. They present no new evidence or insights for our inspection and hence, all other things being equal, they are redundant. The only reason they're retained is to assuage and pacify the existentially timid, who otherwise may lose their bearings and minds when confronted by the brute fact of being orphans in the cosmos. As one co-lecturer told me in Barbados: "If I accepted for one second that only evolution operated, *without the need or governance of a deity*, I'd go kill myself right now!"

Multiply this pathetic response millions of times, and you have the reason atheists are detested so much. We are the nasty "messengers" coming to tell the villagers that their "Emperor" (the deity they believe in) has "no clothes" (doesn't exist). Why wouldn't a happy, more or less content villager not want to kill the messenger after hearing or seeing his pet delusions bushwhacked?

More recently, after one of my columns extolling the Materialist philosophy appeared in the local press, an M.D. wrote in a follow-up letter:

"Depression's etiology is multifactorial and being a theist does not necessarily prevent it.... I remain convinced, however, that the existential impact of living in a Godless universe is a critical component in many people's depression."

If I had the opportunity to confront this M.D., as I did my colleague in Barbados, I'd point out the sheer beauty of nature able to generate novel forms on its own. Why does the absence of a cosmic "store manager" lead to this malaise or depression, while a marvelous and self-sufficient cosmos fails to fill the existential void? Are most humans so pathetically weak and childish that they require 24/7 hand holding by a cosmic super parent? Is that true? If it is, I fear for the future of

---

1.   Jacque Monod, *Chance and Necessity*, 1972, Wm. Collins & Sons, UK, p. 158.

the species. If we're that fragile we won't last even one-millionth the duration of the dinosaurs!

The M.D, like my Bajan colleague and so many millions of humans, seems to require some nebulous Big Cosmic Daddy to watch over the store. But why the need for this father figure? Is it wired into the brain? It must be since the general reaction to atheism is out of all sane proportion to the stimulus. Basically, there's no supernatural Santa! Get over it! Why should that be a reason to hate if I simply tell you the unadorned truth?

In the case of my Bajan colleague, that evolution was underpinned by atheism and chance came as an astounding revelation to him. But it shouldn't have. If one has the fortitude and honesty to look objectively at the theory of evolution, one can easily see that it is unnecessary to postulate or add some kind of additional cosmic "manager."

This security blanket approach of wedding an unnecessary theism to evolution (or accepting evolution but closing eyes and ears and singing: *"La, la, la there's still a god, nothing's denied!"*) I often have compared (in critical thinking lectures I used to give in Barbados) to the efforts to preserve Ptolemaic epicycles by building in minor epicycles to the major ones.

Thus, the additional epicicyles were forced in to preserve the geo-centric cosmos, but at the expense of much simplicity! The easier approach would simply have been to have looked at Tycho Brahe's data (and Kepler's insights), and understand all the complexity vanishes when you just posit the Sun at one focus of an ellipse with the Earth going round it.

But, horror of horrors, there was no room for the deformed ellipse or elliptical orbit in the divinely perfect heavens. After all, only perfect forms could inhabit the vast starry firmament, and such forms had to be circles!

In the same way today, the edict has gone forth that evolution can only occur with the aid of a grand Cosmic Daddy. No way and no how can it unfold on its own, via natural selection, chance and mutation. When, in fact, that is the simplest way possible.

This is a tragedy of imagination and thought compounded by the belief that violence must prevail to abet it. Thus, one reads more and more letters to the Editor of major papers, such as *The Denver Post*, asserting that "atheists need evolution as cover to hide their ungodly beliefs and garner validation for them."

In fact, atheists need nothing of the sort. Evolution stands on its own empirical merits because it can account for vast swaths of biological history through a unifying theme. It also has actual evidence to support its claims, for example in the fossil record of the trilobites, or the horse.

Never mind, hate will out and that hate is directed at atheists since they are the more likely embodiment of support for evolution, as well as all science which "seeks to exclude the supernatural".

To those who would declare themselves atheists, be warned! You'll face such hatred and bigotry wherever you go in this God-besotted land.

2. Why Atheists Are So Disliked in the U.S.

In none of the places I've lived or traveled, even in highly religious third world nations such as Barbados and St. Lucia, have I beheld the venom for unbelievers as in the U.S. It's as if there's absolutely no give, no acceptance or even the most minimal respect afforded. Once you declare yourself an atheist, you are immediately the enemy, and not much better than Osama Bin Laden or one of his cohorts.

Why is this? A first hint of the reasoning has already been given in the previous section. With atheism a whole new way of facing the cosmos is embraced. It relieves reality of supernatural managers, special designs and cosmic purpose.

The bald outcome is that only the most tough-minded rationalists and realists can confront such a universe and thrive in it. For the remainder, fear and chaos threaten, and they're mentally unable to come to terms with a universe minus a Cosmic Controller. Rather than examine the subtext for their own mental and psychological deficiency, they take it out on the "messenger", i.e. the friendly neighborhood atheist!

Two factors drive this: 1) a brain architecture that favors an optimism dynamic and "hope" even when reality testifies to the contrary, and 2) a pernicious culture of "positivity" that reinforces this brain defect, recently highlighted by Barbara Ehrenreich.[2] As Ehrenreich notes, American mass culture is saturated by a saccharine "cult of positivity," with children brainwashed from an early age that they can do anything, and adults brainwashed to believe if they just work hard and long enough they'll become super millionaires like Donald Trump. That no one has slain the insipid "Horatio Alger" myth up to now is really a testament to America's individualist hubris and false optimism.[3]

What has this to do with atheism? Mainly that a culture of positivity will perceive the atheist as an agent of irreversible depression, pessimism and negativity! After all, what could be more of a downer than the notion that all the fun ends once one's physical being expires? When you're dead, you're dead, and there'll be no reruns or afterlives. Factor into this the brain's natural tendency and drive for optimism at any cost, and you have a ready-made cultural and biological axis to deny and thwart atheism! The most expedient way to achieve this is by casting atheism in the most disreputable and inhuman terms possible, and the atheist as little short of a Satanic entity, if not the ugly bearer of mass depression.

Thus, every mental deficiency, perversion and inadequacy in the cultural positivity clique is projected onto atheists. We are the "evil ones." We're the ones trying to "subvert" the grandiose scheme of the country as propounded by the Founders in the Constitution. In fact, that document was intended to keep the state from establishing a religion and to protect the minority from the excesses of the majority.

Many call the U.S. a "Christian" nation, but in reality it is a *faux or pseudo-Christian nation.* It postures Christian beliefs, values and tenets, but hasn't the foggiest clue what they're really about. A recent survey released about American religious beliefs and habits casts the country in a particularly bad light.

The survey noted that fewer than 1 in 4 Americans could name even two authors of the New Testament. A stunning plurality also thought that the phrase

---

2.   Barbara Ehrenreich: "Pathologies of Hope" in *Harpers*, Feb., 2007.
3.   Michael Moore, "Horatio Alger Must Die", in *Dude-Where's My Country?*, Warner Books, 2003, p. 137.

"God helps those who help themselves" came directly from the Bible, rather than the actual author, Benjamin Franklin. More appalling, at least two-thirds believed the saying "Do unto others as you would have them do unto you" came from Jesus, as opposed to the Golden Rule that existed from the time of Hammurabi's Code.

It is fairly clear that this dichotomy between posturing and actual Christian teachings has bred a sense of hypocrisy. It makes sense that this hypocrisy will fuel and reinforce any anger toward outsiders, especially atheists who might have the chutzpah to point it out.

What I'm saying is that in a nation replete with posturing pretenders (or what used to be called "*Pharisees*" in the New Testament gospels), these pretenders will invariably show more anger, rage against outsiders than genuine Christians. This is certainly the case, if one examines closely the American religious tableaux and experience.

By contrast, in Barbados, a nation with more genuinely Christian folk (perhaps because it harbors no military-industrial complex!) I used to experience frequent opposition to my views, but seldom if ever outright hatred and hostility. There was less reason to do so, because the people were more secure in their own beliefs, so that my unbelief didn't bother them.

In terms of greater generality, Barbadians often cite the New Testament injunction that "*whatsoever thou dost for the least of thy brethren, that ye do unto me,*" and they demonstrate it! For example, the nation provides general and accessible health care for all citizens, as well as education and housing. By contrast, the U.S., while proclaiming "Christian values," nevertheless demonstrates a mean-spirited, business-for-profit model health system that denies care to the impecunious (or uninsured) who may most need it, while bankrupting many others that do access it. To add insult to injury, this for-profit model is the most inefficient compared to other advanced nations, delivering the least "bang" for the buck!

In terms of public education, the U.S. has "No Child Left Behind" which actually has the effect of leaving millions behind if their schools' test scores don't measure up, whereupon federal funding can be withdrawn. Exactly, how does this demonstrate the most remote Christian charity?

Another reason the atheist is so disliked in the U.S. is because of the traditional conflation of atheism and communism in the American mass mind. Many people, raised since the odious McCarthy era to detest "godless communism," regard atheists as the next thing to communists. Given that communist-leaning artists and others have always been among the most persecuted in the country (look at the FBI dossiers kept on them[4]) it makes sense that atheists would be convenient secondary targets for this opprobrium.

The events of September 11, 2001 didn't help matters at all, and in many ways introduced a sort of jingoistic McCarthyist religio-regression even more strident than the original brand. While ninety percent or more of Americans sought refuge in their churches and prayer groups, atheists remained unfazed and determined not to be beaten into the fold by strident fear-mongering. Not surprisingly, our patriotism was questioned, since many of us also stood front and center against the illegal pre-emptive invasion and occupation of a sovereign state that had nothing to do with 9/11.

As members of the reality-reason based community, we also knew that al Qaeda had nothing whatever to do with Saddam or Iraq. As for terrorist acts, we knew that statistically they were so remote a possibility as to be no more likely (to befall any given person) than a giant meteor landing from space and crashing into a house or car. But to behold the mounting hysteria and color-coded panic warnings, you'd never know that! Of course, this reign of fear mongering made the repeal of civil liberties (via noxious legislation like the "Patriot Act") much more probable.

Will there ever come a time in America when atheists are respected, if not revered? I don't think so. That would only arrive if we kept our opinions permanently to ourselves, "sat in the back of the civic bus," and behaved like a nice, docile breed of spayed pets. Then, truly, bliss and light would govern the land, but at what cost?

Surely at the cost of the nation becoming ever more inbred with its self-styled and erroneous brand of social Darwinian Christianity, leading possibly to a radical, right wing "Dominion" state in which the Bill of Rights is dead, and democ-

---

4.   Herbert Mitgang.: 1988, *Dangerous Dossiers*, Primus Books.

racy along with it (as well as habeas corpus[5]). A state in which "God" and the Bible are the ultimate authority and sources of any justice delivered.

But all this is hypothetical. No atheist I know has any plans of foregoing his or her free speech rights, and remaining quiet, while right wing religious groups violate the separation of Church and State. And in that case, activist atheists like Michael Newdow will continue to bring court cases to remove "God" in the Pledge, as well as remove it from coinage and keep Ten Commandments displays out of public places. So long as these efforts continue, and they should, atheists can expect to be neither liked nor respected by their mostly zealous, pseudo-religiously indoctrinated countrymen.

3. The Downsides of Closet Atheism

Closet atheism, take it from me, is one of the most comfortable positions for one's psyche in America. No quarrels, no arguments, especially with the immediate family, and one gets along fine with bosses, other acquaintances and the larger society. After all, buttonholed at a cocktail party, it's much more chic to proclaim one is an "agnostic" than an atheist! The term agnostic carries within it a kind of detached, above-it-all wisdom, rather than the total capitulation to feigned ignorance truly at its core.

In my closet years, up until I went public in an article[6], life was fine. I got on famously with my parents, and experienced no problems at work or in the larger community. The publication of the article changed all that, especially with my family.

At first I was constantly berated as a pariah, and reminded that: "no one ever in the family has claimed to be an atheist before you". I was also reminded constantly that my mother was "on her knees" every night saying all the mysteries of the rosary on my behalf. After all, what mother wanted to face the prospect of her oldest son headed for hellfire?

---

5.   Most observers already agree that the "Military Commissions Act of 2006" effectively killed habeas, or at least put it on ice until a courageous Congress can revise the relevant sections.
6.   P.A. Stahl, "My Path to Atheism" in *The American Atheist Magazine*, June, 1992.

After a major family explosion in 1994, which also saw me breaking off communications with a youngest brother, things settled down a bit. However, there were always undercurrents of uneasiness, and constant jabbing and sparring between us over the atheism bogey. The status of the relationship could best be described as "semi-peaceful co-existence," at least ninety percent of the time.

Things weren't better at the corporation where I worked as a tech writer. Almost every morning of every working day, e-mails would arrive on my system with special bible quotes like "the fool hath said in his heart there is no God" and other dreck. Most of the drivel had to do with unbelievers being tossed into a "lake of fire". At one point, on locating the culprit who'd been dispatching these preachy e-mails to me, I threatened to deluge his own e-mail with atheist online tracts. He never bothered me after that.

In the press, people made a big thing of my atheism and tried to use it against me, even to the extent of tying it to a probable lurking socialism. According to one letter writer, my stances on issues were based on a "perverted vision of America as a socialist Nirvana with cradle-to-grave government protections." As I read it I thought: "What the #@%$^& hell is wrong with that?"

Aren't government protections *good*, even cradle to grave? Look again at Barbados for Pete's sake! Look at the plight of the pregnant mom with no job and two other kids to support, or the handicapped guy, or the senior with ravaging and costly illness? Aren't Christians (which the letter writer professed to be) enjoined to care for *"the least of their brethren"*? It looks a bit like stepping through the looking glass when the atheist prefers to have government assume the role of promoting the welfare of the people (see the Preamble to the Constitution) and the Christian believer wishes to repeal it. Obviously this dichotomy is also at the heart of a recent study that found hardcore Christian evangelicals to be the nation's most charitable givers, while secular-liberal types ranked low down.

Of course! Since we (in the latter group) prefer not to let government off the hook for its responsibilities! Responsibilities that inhere in making judicious use of the tax commons, rather then depending on the vagaries of human will in purely voluntary charity.

The right wingers and Christians always seem to forget that phrase in the Preamble of the Constitution to "promote the general welfare," as well as their icon

Adam Smith's famous words (in his 'Wealth of Nations'): "*What improves the circumstances of the greater part can never be regarded as an inconvenience to the whole.*"

A reasonable person is entitled to wonder why anyone would trade a relatively quiet, stable life for all of this grief. The answer is that while one's life and relationships are "stable", because one hasn't outwardly proclaimed disbelief, it is all by way of pretension and posturing. The self-imposed artificiality and ambiguity, in turn, creates no end of mental turmoil and tension because one isn't being true to oneself and one knows it. (What Existentialist Jean-Paul Sartre would call "bad faith"). One is doing what we might call "going along to get along". There are no major battles, violent disagreements, but there is also *no authenticity*. One is, in effect, living a kind of silent lie. What are those famous Mark Twain words?

> "Almost all lies are acts, and speech has no part in them … I am speaking of the lie of silent assertion: we can tell it without saying a word."

So, when one sits amidst god-fearing believers and they come down with a heavy hand of opinion on all atheists, one's silence transmutes to a silent lie. The closet atheist is thereby giving tacit approval to the belligerent and bigoted remarks by keeping his counsel, merely to preserve a social peace.

Then again, there is the loss of affiliation and connection to like-minded people. If one remains "in the closet" then a broader base of kindred folk is forever foreclosed. If no one knows you're an atheist too, why should they relate to you on anything other than a formal level?

I found that while the price of coming out was indeed high, certainly in terms of family relationships, it at once released me from an artificial or contrived universe of choices. My articulated positions could then be more in synch with my actions, my other writings—without contradiction or hypocrisy creeping in. Obviously, however, the choice of whether to declare one's disbelief openly must be personal. At the same time, I can aver that life in the closet is not a life to be proud of, and is more enduring daily a sense of diminution than achieving potential.

4. Other Choices and Euphemisms for the Squeamish

After I sent a copy of my *Atheist's Handbook to Modern Materialism* to my sister-in-law as a gift, she admitted that while she found it interesting she kept the book in a colorful book jacket to conceal its title. This was particularly useful while traveling. I can understand this, because the word 'atheist' is akin to a red flag to many of the general populace. The person carrying around a book marked with this red flag is surely bound to feel the disapproval, not necessarily in overt ways, but definitely in dozens of sundry small ways. Why ask anyone to put up with that?

So, when she informed me of providing a book cover to conceal the title of the book, I perfectly well understood.

In the same way, I can understand anyone who wishes to veer away from the "atheist" label as a means of describing one's unbelief. My wife is like that, though we share extensively the same philosophy and outlook: that the universe is ultimately purposeless, and it is up to each of us to carve our own purpose into the cosmic tapestry. Never mind. She prefers to adopt the less "in your face" term of a freethinker, to my 'atheist and that's perfectly fine.

For those searching for alternative descriptors for their unbelief, the ones listed below might be useful. If not, you may be able to think of a term on your own that describes your own personal niche within the world of unbelievers.

a) Freethinker

This is perhaps the most popular term, because it denotes an underlying positive subtext as opposed to the negative subtext for 'atheist'. Being "free" is good, and so is "thinking". Being a "free thinker", therefore, shows that one enjoys the full latitude of his or her thoughts without being subject to artificial censorship. Certainly, if you ask a thousand unbelievers randomly chosen on the street what they profess to call themselves, I'm fairly sure the plurality will tilt to "free thinker".

The other benefit is that there are many more freethinker societies and clubs scattered across the country, than atheist ones. Thus, say for someone in a backwater of religious conservatism (like I am in Colorado Springs) it's far easier to link up with freethinkers than atheists. (Although many who are in the local free-thinker group are also atheists!)

b) Secular humanist

This term used to be widely popular in the 1990s but for some reason has more and more fallen out of favor. One of the reasons may be that it doesn't really say very much. I mean, anyone for the progress and welfare of humanity (including the use of government tax dollars to provide social safety nets) is clearly a "humanist". Being secular is also no real descriptor, since one might say that the whole of our modern society outside of the religious domain is secular.

More troubling, is the fact that there are religious secular humanists too, who from time to time make their views known. A perfect example of such a group is Americans United for Separation of Church and State. They acknowledge a divine force or deity, but at the same time believe (in accord with the Constitution) that the state must not meddle in religious affairs or promote one religion over another, even indirectly.

Again, there are often many atheists also in secular humanist groups, such as I found when I belonged to the Washington (D.C.) Area Secular Humanists (WASH). But they opt for "secular humanist" because it eliminates having to use the dreadful term "atheist."

c) Eupraxopher:

This term was coined by Paul Kurtz in his excellent book, *Living Without Religion: Eupraxophy.* Though I can see what he's trying to achieve, I somehow don't believe this word will ever come into wide usage, certainly not like freethinker. For one thing, it just doesn't roll off the tongue like freethinker. There is also a great chance that, having told someone that you're an Eupraxopher, ten minutes later he or she will return to ask you:

"What exactly was that you called yourself again?"

This can really get tedious over time. Kurtz must definitely be given an "A" for effort, though.

d) Naturalist:

This is a more recent appellation coined by Paul Kurtz[7], in attempting the age old trick of avoiding definitions forged "by what we are against" as opposed to what we are *for*. This is admirable, again, just like his earlier "eupraxopher," but ultimately fails at the task. It is also confusing since it:

- Makes it more difficult for nonbelievers to identify and network with their fellows

- Conflates a scientific (e.g. from biology) usage with a normative philosophical one

- Flees from an obvious and uncluttered identity rather than embracing it.

Kurtz, of course, would argue with all the above and insist he's attempting to expand the purview of atheism beyond *merely being atheists*! Yes, we are committed to the pursuit of free inquiry, critical thinking and also the scientific process that emphasizes naturalism as opposed to supernaturalism. We also value the application of logic in arguments and discussions, dispassionately presenting our cases to any who would hear. However, all of those represent *necessary conditions* to the core identity that Kurtz (and I'm sure others) seek, and not sufficient conditions.

The sufficient condition is that we disdain and forego any belief in an extra-physical force or intelligence, or invoking such to try to account for physical phenomena and natural laws. This particular sufficient condition makes one an atheist as defined from and take from the ancient Greek usage: *a-theos*, or without God.

In other words, that we may be critical thinkers, "naturalists" or scientists as well is all secondary not the primary criterion by which we are distinguished from the rank and file of humans. Does this define or limit us in terms of what we are against? Possibly, but there is never ever anything wrong or less valued about negative information anyway. This is particularly true when the entity one is set against is ab initio not well defined.

---

7.   Paul Kurtz, *Free Inquiry*, op. cit. p. 4

An example I gave in my first book was the "UFO" seen by hundreds at a shopping Mall in Carol City, Florida in March of 1962[8]. On further inquiry the "object" was *not* an aircraft or weather balloon, *not* a planet or comet or star, and *not* a transient atmospheric phenomenon like ball lightning or an electrical sprite. Since no positive knowledge was available as to what the aerial entity was, *negative information was employed to decide what the entity was not.* For the practicing scientist (and certainly "naturalist" of the Paul Kurtz depiction), negative information concerning a collective set of data or observations is often as important as positive information at arriving at what an entity *is*.

An analogous situation applied to G-O-D. The term is so vague, ambiguous and subjective, that we are only able to say with any degree what it is not, in terms of existing epistemology. By the same token, defining oneself in terms of non-belief or non-investment of intellect is perfectly legitimate. Thus, by accepting and circulating the word "atheist" as applicable to ourselves, we at once signal to others that we don't operate in the realm of miracles, invisible all-powerful Beings, special invisible domains (Heaven, Hell), or secondary invisible agents (demons, angels, souls, Satan). In other words, the very simplicity of usage in conveying our position (in terms of the field of artifacts *omitted*) is what makes the term "atheist" superior to the term "naturalist."

e) Agnostic Atheist

This term is kind of a hedge between using merely the blunt term "atheist" and moderating it with "agnostic". Think of it as a "buffered atheist". Somehow it doesn't come across as cold, or harsh as simply saying "atheist" (again, this is to most of those who have a dislike of all things atheist!) The term was probably first used by George Smith, where he distinguished the various forms of agnostic[9]. As he noted, this form of atheist implies a person who *"maintains any supernatural realm is inherently unknowable by the human mind."*

In other words, even if such domain as the supernatural existed in some ethereal extra dimension of the universe, no one would ever know about it. Thus, it makes no sense to discuss it, or to even acknowledge any kind of 'Supreme Being'

---

8.   *The Atheist's Handbook to Modern Materialism*, 2000, p. 8.
9.   George Smith, *The Case Against God*, Prometheus Books, 1989, p. 9.

within it. Thus, if the supernatural domain is itself "unknowable" than any sub-sets (or supersets) within it are likewise unknowable.

Obviously, if one elects to use this term, then he or she must be aware that it refers to a specific context of atheism. In other words, one isn't necessarily dis-avowing a supernatural entity, only asserting that it can never be known, hence is not worth discussing.

All the above allow some breathing space for the squeamish, those who for one reason or other can't bear the thought of saying they embrace atheism. For my part, however, I will continue to use the term that effectively and concisely says exactly what I do: withhold belief in an unsupportable entity that has no empiri-cal benediction.

That word is ATHEIST!

7

The Three Biggest Challenges to the Atheist

No one can write a basic book on atheism and atheists without considering the challenges posed by living in a culture permeated by religiosity. In the U.S. these challenges are especially great, given how the political system is set up. For example, our "winner take all" election system, with only two major parties, ensures no smaller voices can ever be heard. The most the aspiring atheist can hope for, is to try to get elected at the local level. But even there the chances of success are slim and none. Who, after all, wants to have an avowed atheist on the local school board?

Nevertheless, it is important to address in some kind of positive fashion what the challenges are, and how they might be met. I do not profess to have all the answers here, but base these suggestions mainly on my own experience and that of other atheists with whom I've been acquainted.

1. Finding Self and Voice:

Finding one's authentic self and voice is immensely important if one lives in the U.S. consumer culture—since all values and information have been virtually reduced to the commercial—except for the hyper-religious. What this means is that there is literally minimal civic landscape for the unbeliever, non-corporate citizen to participate.

Democracy in the genuine sense calls not only for votes, but sound reasons why votes are cast, predicated on understanding the competing interests of commercial society, government (more and more tied to the former—via gutted regulatory functions, legalized corporate bribery and payoffs) and civil society.

Atheists, with their own voices and views, must be part of this civil society for it to be authentic.

If the majority simply votes blindly for Ten Commandments' displays, or "moral values" (which is to say, *Christian* wedge-issue moral values) then the rights of the dissenting minority aren't being protected. In this case, reactive ignorance has succeeded in stifling them. This is made worse by the fact that according to a recent poll, 52% of Americans would decline to vote for a "well qualified atheist" for President"[1]

By virtue of such prejudices, of course, an atheist minority can never obtain the full equal protection (as say African Americans) and must be incessantly forced to behold the spectacle of politicos using them to score political points.

What some call "civic space" (which must include the viewpoint of atheists) is where the decisions of average citizens trump big money, corporate lobbies and the revolving door between government agencies and lobbies. At one time, it occupied the middle ground between government and the rapacious commercial-private sector, but because of globalization, is now totally detached. In terms of set theoretics, Fig. 8 represents the situation. with the circle G for government and P for private sector, respectively, with a large intersecting area common to both. The separate circle for civic space or the "set of civic society" is an isolated circle apart from the influence of the previous two.

---

1.   Source: *Mother Jones* magazine, "Faith in the System "Sept.-October, 2004, p. 26.

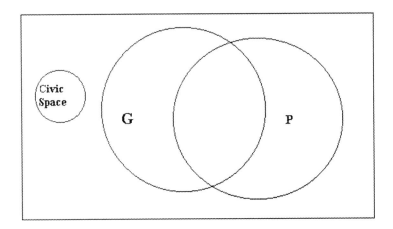

Fig. 9: Set theory depiction of how civic space is now separated from governance.

Note that the intersection of the sets G and P denotes the growing merger between corporate and Government interests. Civic space (C) is where we neither vote nationally (more and more influenced by ad-ism and PR, sound bites) or where we buy and sell. It is where citizens, say in Vermont, converge for public meetings to decide on the location of a homeless shelter, or neighbors pool resources to care for children of low-income workers. Without any government benediction or expectation of commercial sector 'return on investment'. The tragedy today, as seen from your sketch of the three sets, is that as the areas of G and C grow larger, the space available for civic life diminishes.

This is the tragedy of the 20th (and now 21st) century civic commons: The gradual erosion of civil society by government/market interests. Either in pursuit of state (or corporate) power, profits or both. Atheists don't fit into either of these, since their philosophy neither upholds the religious values thatAmerican political interests espouse, or the commodity values that offers return on invest-ment in a market scenario. Hence, they are largely ignored, if not outright excluded, except as consumers. Now the conflation of government and market interests has forced those wishing to live within non-coercive spheres of influence to make a Hobson's choice. They're pressured to either side with state power and "commandeering of individual rights" or ally with private power, and its extirpa-tion of what remains of government.

Choose to be passively serviced (and rendered servile) by a massive bureaucratic state wherein the word citizen has little or no resonance (until it's election time) or submit to the selfishness and barbaric, radical individualism of the private sector—which extols the Social Darwinist refrain of 'survival of the fittest' (only covers it up using the euphemism of the "free market") when there is no such thing. Rather, what we have in the U.S. are either coercive markets, which dictate demand by assorted manipulations, or publicly supported markets (e.g. health care) for which public tax benefits reduce the hazards of competition.[2]

Where does the atheist's self and voice arise in this context? It must emerge within the remaining freedom and latitude of civic space. It must come from feeling confident enough to voice (or write) one's atheist opinions in the local press, or speak at gatherings in order to demonstrate atheists aren't prepared to hide away in dark corners. Even as the Christian reactionaries across the land try to seize control of government and render us second class citizens.

Above all, finding Self must emanate from the choices I described in the previous chapter. Are you (or are you not) bold and courageous enough to call yourself what you are, without invoking euphemism or mollifying words? Are you prepared to act on that identity, and use it to advance the welfare of all unbelieving minorities? The answers here are critical because the finding of Self and Voice typically go together. If you find one, generally you will find the other.

Atheists, now more than ever, need that Self and Voice to re-expand and re-energize civic space in America, to protect it from being occupied as some religious enclave.

2. Where to Project that Voice

A question uppermost in the minds of many atheists, as I've found at atheist conferences, is: Where is the best place to make my voice heard? My answer is always the same: start first in your immediate family, make them aware of the nature of your disbelief, then move out from there. For example, penning letters to the Editor of your local paper.

---

2.   Steffi Woolhandler. and David U. Himmelstein:. *Journal of Health Science*, Vol 21, Issue 4, July-August, 2002.

The most difficult choice I ever made was to articulate my unbelief to my family around 1994. This was made more difficult by the fact that my atheism came as a total shock to them. It was as if they were betrayed at the most fundamental level. Over twelve years of Catholic grade school education, plus High school, and three years of college, for what? That the actual trigger was a lecture given by an Existentialist (Jean-Paul Sarte) *at the Catholic university*, was to add insult to injury?

Following my shocking revelation, more than ten years elapsed in constant parental nagging and arguments, before I managed to elicit a measure of respect. (Though my mother is still wont to get on bended knee and say the mysteries of the rosary for her infidel son). However, it eventually paid off in a relationship predicated on peaceful coexistence. This has now more or less been defined by a policy of "don't say—don't tell". I don't say anything about my unbelief if they refrain from talking about the Catholic Church, or what any of its denizens did or didn't do. I don't care.

After finding my authentic voice in these parental squabbles, I decided to make my views more publicly known, starting with a series of letters to *The Baltimore Sun* through the years, 1995-1999. Most of the letters touched on some aspect of atheism, though they were written (generally) in response to attacks on secular humanism.

When my *Atheist Handbook* was published in 2000, I promoted it on a number of talk radio shows, and often faced off against Christian critics in those venues. Most often the duel ended in a draw, though sometimes I did get the last word in and scored the winning points. In any case, the object wasn't so much to "win" as to be heard, and I was in stations from New Hampshire to California.

After moving to Colorado Springs, the capital of Christian Right America (with its headquarters for 88 evangelical groups) in 2000, I found myself on new, more hostile turf. An atheist entrenched within a dedicated Christian community, whose hero was pretty much James Dobson, the head of Focus on the Family.

Though, naturally, somewhat hesitant at first, I finally came out by agreeing to write on the atheist point of view for The Freethinkers of Colorado Springs, who had a weekly spot in the local independent newspaper. Over the years I wrote over a dozen articles, including these titles: 'Why Materialism?', 'Mind Viruses and Memes', 'The Dogma Delusion', 'Exposing the Hell Myth', 'Evolution Redux' and 'Religious Beliefs and Brain Seizures'. One of the most powerful articles was 'Exposing Civic Ignorance' which was actually a rebuttal to a Christian critic who insisted atheists were "not above being subjected to religious messages from government entities". This followed an earlier letter of mine, in which I compared the Air Force Academy's policies vis-à-vis unbelievers (preventing them from leaving the grounds while Christians could attend prayer meetings, subjecting them to a "Heathen's Run") to those of the Taliban in Afghanistan.

In my rebuttal, since I knew the evangelical Christian locals were big on "the Founders," I cited the words of none other than Thomas Jefferson, in his Bill for Religious Freedom (1779):

> *"To compel a man to furnish contributions of money for the propagation of opinions which he disbelieves and abhors, is sinful and tyrannical."*

Clearly, not everyone will be inclined to write an atheist book, or even do an atheist column. Never mind. That voice can still be projected within your community, say through letters to the Editor, or even by phoning in to a local talk show and airing your views. In either case, other atheists (maybe of the closet type) will see or hear it and not feel so desperately isolated themselves.

3. Preparing for one's demise: wills, memorials, cremations and all that

A recurring bugbear to many atheists is any advanced planning regarding their death. A funeral or no? What about wills, or memorials? There would, of course, be no problem with any of this if death was interpreted as a wholly natural phenomenon that expedites evolution, rather than lathered with all kinds of supernatural mumbo-jumbo and extra baggage. The problem is that in the U.S. that baggage is everywhere, and people in the larger culture tend to question any decisions made that omit the "after life" framework, hence the difficulties for atheists.

Despite the hyper-religious blather with which death continues to be invested, the atheist can still carve out a niche to solve the matter of preparing for his demise. First and foremost is to have a will prepared, and preferably a living will with it. The will basically sets out the distribution of your earthly assets and should be no big deal. Fortunately, there are many accomplished estate lawyers who can help—for a modest fee. There are also "do it yourself" kits available, but I'd advise against it, mainly because the particular estate laws can vary so much from state to state. For example, in Colorado, if the estate holder (i.e. YOU) is deemed "unsound" of mind, a special estate agent can be appointed by the state to oversee (and disburse as s/he sees fit) all your assets. You want to make sure you can do everything possible to prevent such a fate.

More difficult (and controversial, especially following the Terry Schiavo case) is the living will. Since most atheists are Materialists at heart, we also don't want to cling to life if there's no hope or chance of retaining quality. The living will you prepare can insure that you're not kept alive as some kind of vegetable indefinitely, at the behest of modern medicine's wonder devices. The more detailed the will, the more conditions you can set out as to what you will and won't accept for "extenuating circumstances".

Most estate lawyers also have such forms, and as part of the process a check off guide to help in preparing a unique (personalized) living will from a generic template. In my case, by way of example, I requested no special life sustaining devices to keep me going if my EEG shows no brain activity.

Once the matter of wills is settled, you can go on to preparations for disposal of your body, as you see fit. Again, there are a multitude of options available and each atheist will forge a different one depending on his or her particular situation, family ties, and wish to acknowledgement rituals, or otherwise. In my case, I intend to keep it as simple as possible: cremation, with (possibly, depending on the survivors' wishes) a brief memorial, after which my ashes are to be tossed off of Pike's Peak.

My personal belief is that funerals and caskets are a huge waste of money, which only serve to enrich the undertakers. Besides that, cemeteries are a waste of perfectly good space that could be used for something like homeless shelters in the here and now, rather than a redundant abode for decaying corpses.

If I had my 'druthers, I'd do away with any memorials as well, but as my wife has pointed out, sometimes one also has to also think about what others want. I concede that, hence leave that part open. I won't be around in any case to complain!

Obviously, and under no circumstances, should an atheist and his family allow undertakers, relatives or anyone else to mount guilt trips: say over the cheapness of the farewell, lack of coffin or other peripheral arrangements. My response is 'Who cares, already?'

When I'm gone, I'm gone. It makes far more sense, and is vastly more humane, to depart this world without leaving my loved ones mounds of debt to get out from under, or leave them with fewer assets than they might have had, had I not demanded a twenty-four carat sendoff!

Some have asked me, at atheist conferences and freethinker meetings, if prayers ought to be allowed at an atheist memorial. My opinion is that in the matter of prayers, or any other vocal manifestations with supernatural overtones, the will of the deceased is to be rigidly obeyed. If the person is an atheist, therefore, it is an insult to utter prayers, no matter how short or cute. To do that is to besmirch and defile the departed atheist's memory. To do something he would never do.

A few words recalling fond memories, or shared experiences is another thing. A few jokes shared, even better. Just leave out the religious bilge. Best of all, have a huge party with all kinds of fixins' to celebrate the life of the atheist now gone to that enormous void of eternal nothingness.

Living in the midst of a religiously manic nation, as I showed, is not always easy. It presents never ending challenges to the atheist, but that is not to say these challenges are insurmountable. With time, foresight and planning, any of them can be met—whether finding one's authentic self or voice, or completing one's earthly affairs.

Resources for Atheists

Websites:

The Atheist alliance
www.atheistsalliance.org

Atheists United:
www.atheistsunited.org

American Atheists:
www.atheists.org

Atheists dot com
www.atheists.com

American Atheist Magazine:
www.americanatheist.com

Books:

Atheist's Handbook to Modern Materialism, The: Philip A. Stahl, Professional Press, 2000.

Created from Animals: The Moral Implications of Darwinism: James Rachels, Oxford University Press, 1991.

Breaking the Spell: Religion as a Natural Phenomenon: Daniel Dennett, Penguin, 2006.

God—The Failed Hypothesis: How Science Shows That God Does Not Exist, By Victor Stenger, Prometheus Books, 2007

God Delusion, The: Richard Dawkins, Transworld Publishers, 2006

Letter to a Christian Nation, by Sam Harris, Alfred A. Knopf, 2006

Religion Explained: The Evolutionary Origins of Religious Thought:, by Pascal Boyer, Basic Books, 2001

The End of Faith: Religion, Terror and the Future of Reason: Sam Harris, W.W. Norton & Co., 2004.

Index

Affirming the Consequent 69
agnosticism 67, 80
Arguing from authority 61

Brahmin 11, 13, 17, 27, 78

Deism 26, 28

Eupraxopher 116

Fatima 85, 86, 87, 88, 90, 91
Freethinker 103, 115

G-O-D 12, 32, 118
God-concept 11, 14, 15, 16, 78, 79
Godel's Incompleteness Theorems 79

Hell 5, 6, 7, 8, 20, 26, 36, 37, 40, 41, 61, 68, 125

Ignotum per Ignotius 53

Michael Persinger 15, 81
Mithras 19

Monod 105, 106
Monotheism 18

naive realism 90
Naturalist 48, 117

Pantheism 20, 21
Pascal's Wager 39, 42

quantum mechanics 21, 24, 26, 28, 57, 90

Red Herring 57
Religious Science 16

Science of Mind 16, 25
Slippery Slope 63
Socinian deity 43
Sol Invictus 10

Theology 16

Yahweh 11, 13, 33, 78
Young hyper-toroid 22

978-0-595-42737-6
0-595-42737-5

CPSIA information can be obtained at www.ICGtesting.com
Printed in the USA
LVOW131704080512

280868LV00005B/192/A